KU-359-231

WILD BIRDS IN BRITAIN

The British Nature Library

is a new Batsford Series which satisfies a wide-spread need. Its volumes are the work of recognised authorities who are also writers of ability and distinction. Though within the scope of a cheap book it is not always possible to cover in complete detail the whole vast range of each subject, it is emphasised that the volumes are planned primarily as attractive and readable introductions to more specialised study, while their photographic illustrations, clearly reproduced to a large scale, recommend them instantly to all nature lovers. *Each book contains* 100 *of these* from the work of the best contemporary nature photographers, in addition to colour plates, and often text drawings, by leading artists.

Demy 8vo, Cloth, 10*s.* 6*d. net each*

Now Ready

WILD FLOWERS IN BRITAIN

By

ROBERT GATHORNE-HARDY and JOHN NASH

Second Edition, revised

WILD ANIMALS IN BRITAIN

By FRANCES PITT

Published by

B. T. BATSFORD LTD.

LONDON & MALVERN WELLS

1 A Golden Eagle striking a Grey Lag

Water-colour Sketch, from an Eye-witness Account, by J. C. Harrison

The British Nature Library

WILD BIRDS IN BRITAIN

By

SETON GORDON

With 2 *Plates in Colour*
and 100 *Illustrations from Photographs*

SECOND EDITION, REVISED

LONDON
B. T. BATSFORD LTD.
15 NORTH AUDLEY STREET, W.1
& MALVERN WELLS, WORCESTERSHIRE

First Published, April 1938
Second Edition, revised, 1943

MADE AND PRINTED IN GREAT BRITAIN
FOR THE PUBLISHERS, B. T. BATSFORD LTD. LONDON
BY JARROLD AND SONS LTD., NORWICH

TO

MY FRIENDS

WHO LOVE THE WILD BIRDS OF BRITAIN

By the Same Author

Thirty Years of Nature Photography
Afoot in Wild Places
Hebridean Memories
The Charm of Skye
Islands of the West
Edward Grey of Fallodon and His Birds
Amid Snowy Wastes
In Search of Northern Birds
Days with the Golden Eagle

Contents

Acknowledgment

THE Publishers must acknowledge their obligation to the following photographers whose work appears in these pages: namely, Mr. W. S. Berridge for fig. 91; Mr. Arthur Brook for figs. 23, 26, 49; Mr. Stanley Crook for figs. 4, 54, 102; Mr. C. Douglas Deane for fig. 59; Mr. and Mrs. Seton Gordon for figs. 46, 47, 48, 51, 52, 61, 74, 77, 78, 84, 86, 87, 88, 90, 93, 98, 99; Mr. A. E. Hick for fig. 94; Mr. Eric J. Hosking, F.R.P.S., for figs. 3, 5, 6, 7, 8, 10, 11, 12, 13, 14, 16, 17, 18, 19, 20, 21, 22, 24, 25, 27, 28, 29, 30, 33, 34, 35, 36, 37, 39, 40, 41, 42, 44, 45, 50, 56, 57, 60, 63, 64, 65, 66, 68, 69, 95, 100; Mr. John Kearton for figs. 15, 31, 32, 38, 55, 62, 67, 83; Dorien Leigh Ltd. for figs. 9, 96; Mr. G. J. H. Moon for fig. 58; Mr. Oliver G. Pike for fig. 43; Mr. Niall Rankin for figs. 2, 53, 70, 72, 76, 79, 80, 81, 97, 101; Lord Revelstoke for figs. 82, 85; Mr. W. H. Spreadbury for fig. 71; Mr. Peter Webster for figs. 73, 75; and Dr. Graf Zedtwitz for fig. 92. The two colour plates (1 and 89) are included by courtesy of the artist, Mr. J. C. Harrison, and Messrs. Williams & Norgate.

2 A Gannet "putting on its brakes" before alighting

3 A Pair of Stone Curlews at the Nest

Introduction

This book, written in the hope that it may foster a love of wild birds, does not profess to be exhaustive, nor a text-book. Critics may find that certain birds are mentioned only cursorily, but this is unavoidable in a work that is merely a general survey, and is strictly limited as to size. It is naturally impossible, also, to include a photograph of every species of bird, or even of every bird referred to; but despite this the illustrations, gathered from the work of our foremost nature photographers, form, I am convinced, as representative a series as is possible within these limits, and one that has not been surpassed in a book of this sort. I should like the reader to notice especially the magnificent study of a pair of stone curlews at the nest. This photograph, the work of Mr. Eric Hosking, is to my mind one of the finest nature photographs ever taken. Note the happy expressions of these very wary and unapproachable birds, and contrast them with the hunted look of birds which have been photographed by cruder methods and are so nervous that they are torn between mother-love and the fear of man and all his contrivances. Mr. Hosking must be an artist in camouflage and in the building of hides as well as in photography.

People say nowadays, "There are too many bird books." That may be true, but it shows that we as a nation are developing our love of birds, and of all wild creatures. While there are few countries in the world so bird-loving as Britain, yet there is still much to be done to encourage a love of wild birds among our people. We have lost the osprey and the sea eagle as nesting species, and there are other rare birds, such as the absurdly tame and trustful dotterel, which seem to be well on the road to extinction in this country. If the dotterel becomes extinct the egg collector will be entirely to blame. There unfortunately exists a class of persons whose chief aim in life is to possess themselves of as large a number as possible of the eggs of our rarer birds. One clutch of eggs is not enough; they must needs find for themselves, or more often than not bribe other people to find for them, as many nests of the rare species as possible. These collectors never content themselves with one egg: the entire clutch is taken, the excuse of the marauders being that if the whole clutch is taken the bird will then lay again. The effrontery of these people is great. They wisely do not tell a credulous public what would happen if another collector came along and also possessed himself of the clutch the bird had obligingly laid after having been deprived of her first. Would she lay a third clutch for a third collector?

This theory that birds will lay a second time if deprived of their first clutch is perfectly sound when applied to many of our common birds, such as the sparrow and the wood pigeon, but is entirely false when applied to some of the rarer birds which are the collectors' quarry. During a lifelong study of the golden eagle I have never known that noble bird lay again when her eyrie has been robbed by a collector. It is unfortunate for the eagle that she is a conservative bird, and lays each year, or each alternate year, in the same eyrie, which becomes so well known to collectors that they arrive at the nearest inn and wait until the eggs are laid.

But collectors are not the only people who need educating as to the beauty and charm of birds. There are certain game preservers who are worse than the worst egg collector. An egg collector rarely kills the bird, contenting himself with the looting of the nest. But the game preserver orders his gamekeepers to shoot from the nest any bird, be it rare or common, which he imagines (and the knowledge these game preservers have of natural history is painfully small) may prey on his game. In many instances the game preserver is defeating his own ends, by destroying the balance of nature and so causing diseases (such as the grouse disease) to ravage his precious game birds. Golden eagles are shot as they leave the eyrie, despite the law of the land, and even the owl and the mouse-hunting kestrel do not escape. The barbarous pole-trap, although illegal, is still in use at the present day.

It is a sad and disquieting reflection that the law can be broken with impunity when the taking of birds' eggs and the shooting, trapping and poisoning of protected birds are concerned. Unless backed by private effort the Wild Birds' Protection Act is of very little use. Much has still to be done to arouse public feeling on the matter. There is too much sentimental talk; too little action. Ladies wearing expensive fur coats attend meetings to denounce fox hunting, yet the trapping of wild animals for their fur and the skinning alive of seal pups for their warm pelts it seems to me are more horrible acts than the hunting of the fox. Protectionists and sentimentalists almost always overstate their case, and because of this they are not taken seriously. What is wanted is a deliberate and restrained effort to educate public opinion to an appreciation of the charm and beauty of our wild creatures—

of our responsibility towards them. I should like to see much more attention paid to the teaching of natural history to young people. The young should be taught to listen for, and record, the song of each bird in the spring; to treat the nests and the wonderfully coloured eggs with reverence; to watch wild animals without rushing at them with sticks and stones; to love and know trees and flowers, butterflies and moths. How much more happy would our young generation be if they were taught thoroughly the joys of nature, her incomparable music and art!

"But," I hear some reader remark, "I thought you said that we are already a nation of nature lovers!" Perhaps that reader's criticism is justified; perhaps I should have written not that we are a nation of nature lovers, but that there are many nature and bird lovers in our nation. I believe that the man who thinks solely of his pheasants or his grouse is rarer than he was thirty or forty years ago. There is a more tolerant spirit abroad, a dawning of the knowledge that there are other admirable forms of life besides game and that, as regards the wild life of these islands, we are the guardians of posterity.

Critics of the nature photographer say sometimes that he is almost, if not quite, as bad as the egg collector, in that his unwelcome attentions cause the bird to desert her eggs. I do not think those criticisms are justified. There are, it is true, unskilled bird photographers—the profession is not immune from its bunglers—but the photographer who by over-hasty preparations or by incompetency in his method of working makes his bird desert her eggs destroys his own chance of obtaining successful pictures and is thus working against himself. It is necessary for the photographer of birds to be, above all things, patient. Haste is fatal. For those who have not attempted the photography of wild birds, but whose love of birds makes them wish to obtain photographs of their home life, it may perhaps be permissible for me to offer a few words of advice, and to give them the benefit of the experiences, of the successes and failures, which my wife and I have had during the past thirty years.

It must first be realised that birds—there are, it is true, two or three exceptions among British birds—are unable to count: they are unable to distinguish between one and two, where human beings are concerned. It is therefore necessary for the would-be photographer when he goes to his hide previously erected near a nest to be accompanied by a companion. The companion stands conspicuously beside the hide while the photographer creeps into it, and after the observer and his camera are in position for the "watch," his companion then must make as ostentatious a departure as possible. The bird has watched two people—recorded in its mind as "danger"—arrive at its nest: it now sees one person—also recorded as "danger"—leave the neighbourhood of its nest. *Provided it has become used to the hiding-place of the observer*, the bird will show its thankfulness by returning with little delay to its eggs or young. "How am I," the reader of these lines may ask, "to set up my hide so that the bird may have little fear of it?" It is mainly a question of patience: of unhurried and careful methods. The hide must be set up (I am presuming that the photographer is using a hiding-tent) first at some little distance from the nest, and gradually moved nearer. This entails much time, and time in these hurrying days is perhaps more precious than it was. But hurried working defeats its own ends and is time wasted.

Sea birds, being comparatively ignorant of man, and therefore less afraid of him, are more easy to photograph than land birds, and many photographs of these birds of the ocean may be obtained without a hide: provided the photographer's movements are slow and unhurried he may approach birds such as the razorbill, guillemot or puffin so as to be only a few feet from them, without causing them much uneasiness.

For those readers who wish to read more deeply of the birds mentioned in this book, there are a number of admirable books on British birds. First among them I should place Witherby's *Practical Handbook*, in which is contained a mine of concise and accurate information on, and a detailed description of, every known British bird.[1] Another work is Coward's *British Birds*, and this can be recommended to all bird students.

Lord Lilford's *Birds of the British Islands*, in seven volumes, is remarkable because of its beautiful coloured plates by A. Thorburn, but it is a rare and valuable work which may perhaps best be consulted in some public library.

Thorburn is no longer with us, but the beauty of the form and colouring of birds is faithfully shown at the present day in the paintings and sketches of men such as Peter Scott and J. C. Harrison.

A love of birds is no superficial and transient thing: it will remain an oft-recurring blessing throughout the life of the lover, so that, wherever he may find himself, he will never be lonely. For, as the Gaelic proverb has it, "Deserted indeed is that country where no voice of bird is heard."

[1] A new and enlarged edition in five volumes is now in the press.

4 Rooks building

5 A Greenfinch and Young

CHAPTER I

Garden Birds

THE *house sparrow* is given first place in this chapter, not because it is an admirable bird, but because it is present in almost every garden in the British Isles. The house sparrow is of all birds the least attractive, and is to a great extent parasitic on man. Even the late Viscount Grey of Fallodon, one of the greatest bird lovers we have had, in a letter to a correspondent writes: "No bird should be shot, except the sparrow, which in the country is very mischievous, and makes itself a nuisance to men and other birds." That indeed is no under-statement. The house sparrow appears to delight in wanton mischief. Rock gardeners know from sad experience how sparrows fly down on to the rock garden and tear off the petals from the delicate Alpine plants. One summer sparrows tore off almost all the petals from the first red rose to open in our garden in the Isle of Skye. Vegetable gardeners know to their cost the destructiveness of the house sparrow. Young peas are torn out by the roots and much damage is done to other young plants also.

At the beginning of harvest the house sparrows sometimes leave the gardens for the fields, and there they eat quantities of standing grain. They perch upon the straw and quickly pick out the grain, and as they have voracious appetites, a large flock of house sparrows may work a great amount of mischief in a corn-field in a short time. The destructiveness of the London sparrow may be seen any spring in the London parks. In St. James's Park fields of crocuses delight the eye on the young green grass on March days. The park authorities endeavour to protect these flowers from the sparrows by a network of thread which in theory should trip up the marauding birds, and prevent them destroying the crocuses. Yet in reality these threads are of little use, and any park frequenter may see the flowers of crocus torn by the sparrows, mainly to expose the honey at the base of the stamens, but partly because of a sheer love of destruction.

But the misdeeds of the house sparrow do not end here. It

is a bully to all other small birds, and upon occasion is not above sucking and breaking their eggs. The graceful martin, which nests beneath the eaves, falls an easy victim to it. The martin's beautifully fashioned nest of mud is too tempting for a sparrow to resist. I have watched a house sparrow deliberately wait until the martin's nest was almost completed, and then take possession of it. There must be some objectionable smell about a house sparrow, for if a sparrow enters a martin's nest for even a few minutes, this is sufficient to cause the rightful owner to forsake it. It would appear that the house sparrow carries with it a slum odour, offensive to the martin, which is an aristocrat among birds. In this indictment I do not include the tree sparrow, distinguished by its black patch on the ear coverts and its chocolate crown. The tree sparrow is a scarce and retiring bird.

The *starling* is as ubiquitous as the sparrow, yet has a very different character. The sparrow is indolent and parasitic: there is no harder-working nor more independent bird than the starling. Watch a family of starlings on your lawn. Their search for food is nothing less than feverish: it is apparent that each moment for them is of supreme importance. Repeatedly they thrust their bills into the grass, and the careful observer will notice that the mandibles of the bill are open during the thrusts. The mandibles may be sensory, and when open are able to "feel" more ground, or they may be held open in order to grasp the more readily any edible prize that may be discovered. It is little wonder that, being so hard-working and adaptable, the starling should be increasing almost everywhere. It is not a destructive bird, yet may acquire a taste in strawberries which makes it a nuisance in a garden. Its habit of building its nest in a chimney is also an unfortunate one, as is its habit of fouling the ground beneath the trees in which it roosts. The starling is a wholly self-reliant bird, and is not, like the sparrow, dependent for its increase on the human race. It may indeed nest in a chimney, or in a hollow tree in a garden, but it is equally at home on some uninhabited Hebridean island where it nests, sometimes with puffins, in crannies among the boulders. In winter, starlings roost in large flocks on small uninhabited Hebridean islands. Near to my home in northern Skye are two such islands, and each morning of winter the starlings from the isles may be seen flying in strongly from the Minch to their feeding ground, and, as dusk

6 A Song Thrush bringing Food to the Nest

7 A Starling at its Nesting Hole

8 A Hen Blackbird at her Nest in wire netting

9 A House Martin at the Nest

is falling, winging their way in a compact flock out over the stormy Minch to where their isle with its roosting cave rises dimly on a storm-vexed sea. The peregrine falcon sometimes chases these starling flocks, but rarely is seen to stoop at one in earnest; starling flesh is believed to be unappetising to falcons and hawks.

The City of London, as every bird watcher knows, shelters each winter a population of tens of thousands of immigrant starlings. These starlings, many of which come from Germany and the lands which border the Baltic, may be seen flying back from the country each winter afternoon as dusk is settling over London. They are undeterred by the smoke and the fogs and may be seen dropping in great flocks from the murky sky as they dive towards such well-known roosting-places as the National Gallery, Charing Cross station, and the wooded island on the lake of St. James's Park. A very different roosting-place is chosen by the starlings of the Outer Hebridean island of North Uist. These birds roost in a reed bed of a loch, and as they arrive at sunset the sound of their wings is like the distant music of the surf on a lonely storm-bound shore.

The starling, with metallic sheen of greens and blues on its plumage, is a handsome bird, and were it less numerous and plebeian its beauty would be the more appreciated. Its eggs, too, are of great beauty, and the delicate unspotted blue of the shell is seen at its best when the egg is new-laid.

The usual song of the starling is unambitious, and without great musical value, but the bird is an accomplished mimic, and will copy with faithfulness the notes, and the song, of almost any bird. In curlew country it may be heard to give a soft imitation of the curlew's cry, and in the Hebrides I have heard it imitate the whimbrel so cleverly that at first I was completely deceived. In gardens it sometimes gives a brilliant imitation of the song thrush's notes.

Occasionally, in autumn or winter, a starling with a crest and with rosy-pink breast, back, and flanks, may be seen. This is the rose-coloured pastor, or rose-coloured starling, an immigrant from south-east Europe, which has not, so far as is known, ever nested in this country.

Few gardens in Britain are without their *song thrush*, known usually in Scotland as the mavis. From Land's End to the farthest Hebrides the song thrush makes sweet music by day and also by night—for in the Hebrides the thrush at midsummer habitually sings until eleven o'clock, and I have one record, from Harris, of a song at 11.20 p.m.[1] Fortunate are the British Isles that so sweet a singer should be so numerous.

Many poets have sung of the melody of the song thrush. Robert Browning, in his immortal lines:

> That's the wise thrush; he sings each song twice over
> Lest you should think he never could recapture
> The first fine careless rapture!

seems to me to bring before the mind the most perfect vision of the song of the mavis, heard perhaps in the soft air of a summer dawn or when the last glow of the sunset is fading from the western sky. We look upon the song thrush as a part of a British garden; we think of the bird living a quiet and rather uneventful life in, or near, that garden. Many of us would be surprised to hear that some—though not all—song thrushes are great wanderers. Many British song thrushes winter in Ireland, France and Spain, and their places are taken by thrushes from the Continent, which are rather greyer in colour than our own birds. These Continental thrushes haunt our shores and open spaces rather than the woods. Mr. R. M. Lockley informs me that on North Ronaldshay in the Orkney Isles many thrushes, as well as other immigrant species, meet their death by striking the glass of the lantern of the lighthouse there, and that the island sheep eat them, consuming first the head and feet, and the body at a later date when it has become partially dried.

Like other song birds, thrushes vary in the quality of their music. Competition or rivalry—call it what you will—is as stimulating for birds as for men, and a lonely song thrush is rarely a first-class singer. The best songsters have almost always rivals to sing against. Like the starling, the mavis on occasion mimics the notes of other, and sometimes unexpected, birds. I once heard, in a pine forest near an eagle's eyrie, a thrush repeating clearly the loud yelp of a golden eagle. On another occasion I was surprised to hear, in the most unlikely surroundings, the flute-like cry of a greenshank coming almost from my feet. The notes were so perfectly reproduced that it was some time before I could realise that they were made by a Hebridean song thrush singing, as is customary with that species, on a rocky ledge beside the tide-swept Minch.

The homely *blackbird*, or merle, begins his song rather later

[1] This is by Single Summer-Time.

in spring than the thrush—which indeed in some districts sings throughout the winter. There are, it is true, reports and letters to the newspapers each year of blackbirds' songs in January, but almost always the letters come from those unpractised in bird song, who have mistaken the mistle thrush's song for the blackbird's. The blackbird is rarely heard in song until the end of February and, perhaps because he begins to sing later than the thrush, is heard in July when the thrush is silent.

The blackbird is a less bold singer than the thrush: his song is more intimate but is no less sweet. The song thrush sings measured, stately phrases: the blackbird's music is more of a warble. Bird lovers from abroad who are unfamiliar with the blackbird's song are impressed by it. When President Theodore Roosevelt visited Britain Sir Edward Grey (later Viscount Grey of Fallodon), Secretary of State for Foreign Affairs, took him in spring for a long day's walk through the New Forest. Lord Grey told me that the President on hearing the blackbird's song was deeply impressed. He could not understand why the people of Britain did not fully appreciate the beauty of that song. Admirers of the blackbird say that his song is finer than the nightingale's. Like the song thrush, the blackbird varies greatly in the quality of his song, and he, too, sings best where rivalry and competition are keen.

It is strange that the blackbird, not content with building the same mud-lined nest as the song thrush, should add a final lining of straw and dried grass above the mud, and on this should lay the four or five eggs closely freckled with red-brown on a bluish-green ground.

Like the thrush, the blackbird is an autumn and winter migrant to many parts of Britain. In the treeless district of northern Skye, where the blackbird rarely nests, a large immigration takes place in early November, probably from Scandinavian countries.

The *robin*, because of its fearlessness, occupies a warm place in men's hearts. It has supreme confidence, knows what it wants, and generally gets it. At Fallodon, Lord Grey tamed the robins of the place, so that they flew down and fed from his hand; in the last year of his life a robin, after being fed, used to fly on to his hat and sing there. Another robin in winter was accustomed to haunt the greenhouse at Fallodon, and to fly down from its hiding-place amid sweet-scented plants to be fed.

The robin is one of the few British birds to sing in autumn, and the song, when heard on a still October day when the leaves are falling softly after a night of frost, has a melancholy quality, as though the bird sang for summer days that are gone.

We all know the old legend of the babes in the wood, and how they were covered over with leaves by the robin. But the robin I saw on the Cairngorm Hills some years ago had no one to perform this kindly office for it. It was April, and the snow lay very deep on the high hills, as it often does in spring. Two friends and I had climbed to the watershed of Lairig Ghru, that high hill pass which leads through the heart of the Cairngorms. All was white: even the great boulders were invisible beneath the deep covering of snow, on which the ptarmigan was the only living thing to be seen. Near the Pools of Dee a small dark speck was seen on the snow. We walked up to it, and found to our surprise a robin lying lifeless on that virgin surface. Robins from the Continent visit Scotland in considerable numbers each winter, and it is probable that this bird had flown, on migration, into a snow blizzard while crossing the Cairngorms and, choked by the drift, had met its death here. When mist and drifting snow cover the Cairngorms it is probable that more bird tragedies occur than are generally realised, and I have found, at a height of almost 4,000 feet on Ben MacDhui, the mummified remains of a lapwing which had perhaps met its death in this way.

The *chaffinch*, like the robin, is found in most British gardens, and, because of his cheery presence and his rollicking song, is deservedly popular. Long ago, as a boy, I used to compare the song of the chaffinch in different districts. At this time I was living in Aberdeenshire, and from careful observations I found that the song of the chaffinch varied in each few miles of the valley of the Aberdeenshire Dee—the song at Aberdeen would be different from the song at Aboyne, and the song at Aboyne different from the song at Braemar. Yet in each district the song would be constant—you could tell at once a Braemar chaffinch, or an Aboyne chaffinch.

Swallows, martins and swifts are garden, or perhaps rather house birds. They make their home with man, yet considering how close to him they live are curiously aloof from him. The *swift*, after it has lived for three months in a cranny above your bedroom window, one morning in early August takes its departure for Africa with never a word of good-bye: the next day that swift may be hawking flies above the south-west coast

10 A Wren

11 A Robin

12 Garden Warblers feeding their Young

13 A Great Tit at the Nesting Hole

of France. The martin and the swallow are more friendly, yet they, too, are wholly independent of man, except in so far as he provides them with a shelter for their nests. This spirit of detachment is perhaps explained by the fact that neither swifts, swallows, nor martins are in the least dependent on man for their food, and so, in a way, their presence about his house and garden is the more delightful.

The swift is found, not only in country places, but in towns and cities. Above the heart of Edinburgh, or of Glasgow with its million inhabitants, swifts may be seen of a fine summer's evening tirelessly wheeling. Towards sunset the swifts, descending from a height, dash madly around the church steeple, or house, where they nest, uttering a harsh, long-drawn scream as they pass, at the speed of an express train, the entrances to the crannies where their mates are perhaps listening to this music with appreciation. As the light fades the swifts mount again into the high air and are no more seen, and it has been suggested that they spend the short summer night at vast heights, sleeping on the wing. M. Jaques Delamain, in support of this, mentions that an airman, flying above the clouds at 10,000 feet during the Great War, passed one night many swifts floating apparently asleep with motionless wings. Although the swift is so finished an artist in flight it is helpless should any mischance place it on the level ground. Its wings are so long, and its legs so short, that it is unable to rise, and if not assisted into the air remains helplessly on the grass until it becomes numbed by the cold night air or is taken by a cat. Because of this inability to rise from the ground[1] the swift must eat and drink always on the wing, and must even gather its nesting material while in full flight.

Although the swift usually is seen near human habitations, it often flies in fine summer weather up to the high hills. I have seen many swifts sailing across and above the great precipices of Lochnagar, at a height of almost 4,000 feet above sea-level, and an observer reports that he saw one of these swifts carrying nesting material in its bill, so there is the possibility that some of the birds may even nest at this great height, as does the Alpine swift on occasion on the hill ranges of the Continent.

The *swallow* is, if the term be allowed, a more homely bird than the swift. Its nest also is more accessible, for it is placed usually on the rafters of cow-sheds and other out-buildings.

[1] This I have proved, although I understand that instances are on record of swifts rising from the ground.

Last summer I was able, by standing up in my car, to feel the eggs in a swallow's nest in a low shed that at the time was being used as a garage. The swallow may be distinguished at a glance from the martin by its long outer tail feathers and (at closer quarters) its chestnut-red throat and forehead, and by the lack of the snowy white rump that is so conspicuous in the martin.

Poets through the ages have sung of the swallow: Chaucer, nearly six hundred years ago, wrote of "the swallow, mortrer of the flyes smale." Its long journey each autumn from Britain across the Equator to South Africa was not then known, nor indeed was it realised for many years afterwards. It was thought that swallows and martins hibernated in holes in walls and mud banks and indeed in some districts the belief still lives. James Thomson, in the early eighteenth century, had this belief in his mind when he wrote:

> When Autumn scatters his departing gleams
> Warn'd of approaching Winter, gathered, play
> The swallow-people; and tossed wide around,
> O'er the calm sky, in convolution swift,
> The feathered eddy floats: rejoicing once,
> Ere to their wintry slumbers they retire;
> In clusters clung, beneath the mouldering bank,
> And where, unpierced by frost, the cavern sweats,

and there are many old accounts of the swallow-tribe being found, by the crumbling of some bank or wall, deep in their winter sleep. Experts will tell us that it is impossible for a swallow; or indeed for any bird, to hibernate, yet the theory is a fascinating one, and that birds do on occasion become torpid during cold has been proved by finding swifts in an arctic May numbed and unable to fly, in the nesting crannies where they had crept for warmth.

The *martin*, often called the house martin, nests usually under the eaves of houses, but I have seen its colonies on sea cliffs. It arrives in this country later than the swallow, and as it often rears two broods it is found nesting late in summer. I have indeed seen martins feeding their young in the nest in bitter October weather, when insect food must have been very hard to find. The nest of the martin is a work of art, and so skilled is this winged mason that its home may stand for years.

Both martins and swallows gather in flocks before the autumn migration, and sometimes fly south in company.

Of the sand martin I shall write in a later chapter.

The *wren*, one of the smallest of British birds, rejoices in a vast scientific name—none less than *troglodytes troglodytes troglodytes*. Although it is found in almost all British gardens the wren is a retiring little bird: there is a mouse-like quality in its sudden disappearance in walls and behind bushes. Its short tail is usually perkily upturned and it is a most active bird although it does not perhaps wander far. When singing the wren produces so full a volume of sound that the song has been called "shattering." The wren sings not only in spring but throughout the winter. The cock wren is so skilled an architect that he builds several nests, which he uses to sleep in: they may be distinguished from the lady wren's nest by the fact that they are not lined with feathers. The St. Kilda wren, found only on the St. Kilda group of islands, has a more melodious song than the common wren: it is a rather larger bird and the bill is thicker and stronger.

Those of us who have bird tables are very familiar with the *titmouse* family. As representative of the garden titmice I take the blue titmouse, the coal titmouse and the great titmouse. The cobalt blue crown of the blue tit at once distinguishes it from the coal tit, a bird of somewhat similar size with black head and white cheeks. The great titmouse can be recognised by its large size, and the broad black band down the yellow breast. Hundreds, nay thousands upon thousands, of coconuts must each winter be hung up in British gardens for the titmouse family. It is believed that a diet of unrelieved coconut is bad for a tit's digestion, and it is well therefore to fill coconuts with dripping, and to hang up suet and peanuts as a change of food.

When the warm sunlight of April bursts the buds of the larch and birch, so that the air is fragrant with their perfume, the bird lover thrills to hear a sweet and plaintive cadence of song that drops earthward from a singer invisible in leafy boughs. Like Beethoven's music, that song seems to come from another world. The singer is the *willow warbler*, newly arrived from a long overseas journey, undertaken with no guide nor chart nor compass, often in the face of adverse winds and storms. Could the little bird tell us of his adventures, what a thrilling story they would make: how great a contrast is his singing-place from the great Atlantic combers off the Land's End which he so recently passed. Soon the domed nest, lavishly lined with feathers, will be built in the long, rough grass, and six or seven fragile red-speckled eggs will be laid. In appearance the *chiffchaff* closely resembles the willow warbler, but in song is at once unmistakable. "Chiff-chaff, chiff-chaff, chiff, chiff-chaff, chiff" proclaims to all who the singer is.

The *hedge sparrow* or dunnock is a self-effacing bird; even its plumage is sombre and inconspicuous. It is a dainty feeder and is able to find food on ground where other birds have searched for it in vain. The hedge sparrow's eggs are of a lovely unspotted blue, and the nest is placed usually in a thick bush or shrub. That beautiful bird the *bullfinch* is unpopular because of the havoc it works in an orchard when cherries, pears, apples and other fruit-trees are coming into flower. It is one of the most confiding of British birds, and on one occasion I tamed a hen bullfinch so thoroughly that she would fly off the nest and take hemp-seed from my hand, and even from my lips. Her young were unable to understand her behaviour, and it was interesting to see them shrink in terror deep down in the nest while their mother flew fearlessly up to me and perched on my hand. The *greenfinch* is perhaps noticeable mainly because of the strange love flight of the male bird, who moves, always in full song, in swift erratic flight through and above the trees and bushes of the garden.

The *blackcap's* song is usually poured forth from dense cover. It is a beautiful song, of rich and varied melody, modulated with a master touch. The song of the garden warbler, "a continuous sweet and mellow warble," is softer and less varied than the blackcap's music.

It may be fitting to take as the final example of a bird of the garden the *spotted flycatcher*, a bird grey in colour and unmistakable in its behaviour as it flies from its perch to capture some insect and returns again to the same perch. From its winter quarters in South Africa the spotted flycatcher travels leisurely northward and arrives in Britain seldom before mid-May. I remember as a boy my pleasure each summer on seeing the pair of flycatchers which used to nest year by year in a shallow hollow in a dead limb of a birch-tree. How often did I visit the tree to satisfy myself that the birds had indeed begun to build! It was surprising that my frequent disturbances did not make the flycatchers desert their nest.

14 A Cock Blackcap at the Nest

15 A Hen Bullfinch at the Nest

16 A Long-tailed Tit bringing food to the Nest

CHAPTER II

Birds of Woodland and Hedgerow

THE woodlands of Britain hold, summer and winter, a great population of birds. In some Continental countries song birds are trapped and shot as delicacies for the table, but in Britain we are more fortunate, although the trapping and snaring of song birds still goes on in certain districts.

In April and May, when birch and beech, larch and elm, hide their boughs in a mist of most delicate green; when the young leaves of the oak are a glowing bronze and the gorse in woodland clearings lies to the sun like a living flame, then songs of happy birds arise, and the perfumed air is filled with gladness.

A book might be written on woodland birds alone. In a single chapter—all that is allowed to me in the present volume—it is not possible to describe at all fully the woodland and hedgerow birds of our country.

It is perhaps right that I should give pride of place to the *nightingale* who, as Milton has it, "all night tun'd her soft layes." Those magic lines of Keats must have found an echo in many a heart:

> Thou wast not born for death, immortal Bird!
> No hungry generations tread thee down;
> The voice I hear this passing night was heard
> In ancient days by emperor and clown:
> Perhaps the self-same song that found a path
> Through the sad heart of Ruth, when, sick for home,
> She stood in tears amid the alien corn;
> The same that oft-times hath
> Charm'd magic casements, opening on the foam
> Of perilous seas, in faery lands forlorn.

There are those who say that the nightingale's song has been overrated: that the song of the blackbird is fully its equal. It is perhaps invidious to compare critically two beautiful things, and it will not, I think, be disputed that one of the charms of the nightingale's music is that it is heard during the silent watches of the night, when song thrush and blackbird are asleep. Milton writes that the nightingale "Sings darkling, and in shadiest covert hid, Tunes her nocturnal note." Jacques Delamain, the poet-naturalist, thus writes of the nightingale:

"By what caprice of Nature has the nightingale chosen to woo his mate and sing her praises in the darkness? His close cousins the Robin and the Redstart love to linger in the twilight and begin their songs again in the first morning light, but his inspiration comes at ten in the evening. Perhaps it is merely that the songs of the day are over, and all things enfolded in silence and mystery, that his voice sounds so full and so finely varied. But what other voice from a bird's throat could compose such a strain, with its beautifully modulated trill and its single note repeated and enhanced in a phrase for us so charged with emotion? Wherever the Nightingale dwells, from Asia Minor to the Atlantic, no song of nature save perhaps that of the Lark, has so stirred the heart of man. Poets have interpreted it, fables been inspired by it. To some it speaks of the joy of spring and the serenity of its nights. We no longer imagine, as did the Greeks, that it tells of despair, but its accent of desire and hope and prayer touches us far more than any expression of mere joy."

And yet in appearance there is nothing distinguished about the nightingale: it is an insignificant small brown bird, about the size of a robin.

The nightingale is a bird of the night—although indeed it may sing long and well during the brilliant hours of an early summer day also.

The *mistle thrush* or storm cock, known by early writers as the mistletoe thrush from the belief that the young were fed only on the berries of the mistletoe, is a lover of full daylight. It was believed that the seeds of the mistletoe, held sacred by the Druids, were transplanted from one tree to another by the mistle thrush. This thrush, the largest of our song birds, is found throughout the British Isles. His song is loud and wild, a single phrase repeated again and again. The mistle thrush's song has a quality of impatience and of defiance; the pauses between the phrases are abrupt, and after a brief silence the song falls again suddenly on the ear, in its full power. There is a stately measure in the music of the song thrush; the blackbird's flute-like song flows easily, like some moorland stream; the song of the storm cock is a song of strength, a challenge to all the world beneath his lofty singing perch, on the topmost bare bough of a high tree, bent by the January gale.

In an open winter the mistle thrush begins his singing before December is out: he sings best when the wind is strong from the west—an Atlantic wind, soft and warm, that brings moisture from the ocean far over the land. Mistle thrushes migrate after the nesting season, and I have frequently seen them at 4,000 feet above sea-level on the high plateaux of the Cairngorm Hills, where no tree is to be found.

The *tree creeper*, unlike the mistle thrush, is a self-effacing bird. Its life is spent climbing with marvellous ease the vertical trunks of woodland trees in its hunt for insect food. Its claws are long and strong, and its tail is pressed against the bark as an aid to its climbing. The creeper can run up a tree a good deal more easily than a man can run across the street. When it has hunted one tree to its satisfaction it flies down to the foot of the tree next it and searches it too with thoroughness. Tree creepers are happy to roost in the crevices of the rough bark of *Wellingtonia sempervirens*, the Californian redwood tree, which grows well in Britain, and by visiting these roosting crannies after dark with an electric torch it is sometimes possible to find these small birds as it were tucked up in bed, and cosily asleep.

The *nuthatch*, another expert tree climber, unlike the tree creeper does not use its tail as a help in climbing, and feeds on nuts rather than insects. It is able to descend trees and walls head downwards, which the tree creeper cannot do—or at all events never does. In flight the species is unmistakable, for its very short tail, stout head, and strong bill give it, as it flies with a slow and undulating motion, a different appearance to any other British bird. It is a dweller chiefly in south and central England, and is rarely seen in Scotland. At certain bird-tables it is a regular visitor.

The *tree pipit* is delightful because of his song. Flying almost vertically into the air from the topmost bough of some tree, the bird floats earthward, the while uttering his pleasing little song—wild and rapid and ending in the calls—"see-ar, see-ar, see-ar," before coming again to rest on his perch. The tree pipit is very like the meadow pipit, but is rather larger, and the tail is longer. It is a summer migrant, and it is usually May before it reaches us from its winter home in Africa. Its favourite haunts are areas of open woodlands.

The *redstart* is often found in the same country as the tree pipit, but it is seen also in denser woods. One highland glen I know where ancient pines and birches clothe the banks of a foaming hill torrent. Here, when the buds of these old birches are at length bursting, a bird with a bright chestnut-red tail (which perhaps because of its bright colouring appears unusually long), pure white forehead and copper-red breast, may be seen flitting from tree to tree: when it pauses from these flights its tail trembles and quivers in a curious manner. This is the male redstart, one of the most handsome of our smaller British birds, newly arrived from his winter quarters in Africa. In his happiness in reaching home once again the redstart often sings his short, rather liquid song, which seems to end with unexpected abruptness, as though the singer had been alarmed and had stopped short in his vocal efforts. The lady redstart, who also has a red tail, lays her delicate eggs, of a pale unspotted blue, in a hole in a tree, and when the brood are hatched both parents are most anxious when danger threatens, often uttering the alarm note, a hurried "whee, tic-tic."

The *wood warbler* is a small, inconspicuous bird with a tremendous song. This song is usually accompanied by a shivering and a shaking of the small wings, as though the singer had worked himself into an ecstasy. He is indeed a true operatic singer. The wood warbler resembles the willow warbler and the chiffchaff, but the breast is sulphur-yellow, and the species is rather larger in size. The nest is domed like a willow warbler's nest, but there is no lining of feathers to it.

The *yellow hammer* or yellow yeorling or yellow bunting is found almost everywhere throughout the British Isles. It is essentially a bird of the hedgerows. Its yellow head and its characteristic song, which has been put into human words as, "A little bit of bread and no che-e-ese," make it one of those homely birds that gladden the heart of the traveller when he or she returns to this country after a prolonged absence abroad. The characteristic eggs, with their fine hair-like markings of dark brown (typical of the bunting family), the dainty nest that is usually lined with horsehair, the prolonged breeding season—I have seen small young in the nest in September—all these things are typical of the yellow hammer. In winter yellow hammers frequent the corn-stacks and farmyards along with sparrows, greenfinches and chaffinches.

17 A Cock Redstart

18 A Cock Nightingale at the Nest

19 A Wood Wren at the Nest

20 A Mistle Thrush with her Young

There is a curious old saying that:

A brock, a toad, and a yellow yeorling
Drink a drop o' the deil's blood
Every May morning.

In the last chapter I have written of those titmice which may be said to be garden-haunting birds. In that chapter I omitted four species, as they seemed to me to be birds of the woodlands rather than of the garden. The four species are the crested titmouse, the long-tailed titmouse, the marsh titmouse and the willow titmouse.

The *crested titmouse* is a very local bird. At its main nesting country, the old pine forests of the valley of the upper Spey[1] the crested tit is by no means rare, but each season egg collectors rob scores of nests of the species, and so far no means has been found of enforcing the Wild Birds' Protection Act. The crested titmouse usually excavates its own nesting hollow. This hollow is made near the base of a decayed pine stump, and the digging out of the hollow, and the fashioning of the nest inside it, may occupy several weeks. The conspicuous crest, the guttural scolding notes, and the greenish, dusky colouring, at once distinguish the crested tit from other titmice. It does not leave its pine forests throughout the year, and in winter accompanies the hind-stalker without fear, for it feeds on the fat which is a part of the *gralloch* of the animal which has been shot.

The *long-tailed titmouse* is distinguished by its long tail and its delicate fairy-like flight. The domed nest, woven together with cobwebs and a little hair, and slung in some lichen-covered tree or bush, is a work of art, and in the lining of the nest more than two thousand feathers have been counted. Eight to twelve eggs are laid by the long-tailed tit, and the large family are united by a strong bond of affection, and keep together throughout the summer and autumn months, often haunting birch woods, where they feed on minute insect life.

When brooding, the long-tailed tit disposes of her long tail by bending it backward, so that it sometimes emerges above her head from the small hole which is the entrance to the nest.

The *marsh titmouse* and the *willow titmouse* closely resemble one another. Both species can be distinguished from the coal tit by the absence of the white patch on the nape of the neck.

The marsh tit has the crown of the head a glossy blue-black; the crown of the willow tit is a dull sooty black. The willow

[1] A number of these forests are alas (1943) being felled.

tit seems to replace the marsh tit in Scotland, and is found nesting in the Spey valley. The marsh tit sometimes comes to the bird table, but I do not think that the willow tit has ever been recorded as doing this.

The *golden crested wren* is best known because of its diminutive size, and because of its beautifully constructed small nest, which is slung like a tiny hammock from an upper bough of some coniferous tree. It is hard to think of so small and fragile a bird crossing each autumn in great flocks from Scandinavia to this country above the waters of the stormy North Sea, yet each year many thousands make that long and perilous journey, and many meet their death at sea or by striking themselves against the strong glass of some lonely lighthouse, to which they have been attracted by the dazzling brilliance of the light. This tiny bird has a dainty high-pitched song, very delicate and sweet.

The *pied flycatcher* in its strongly contrasted black and white plumage is a conspicuous bird, a summer visitor like the spotted flycatcher, but very local in its nesting haunts. I have watched pied flycatchers at their nesting-places in the birch and alder woods of hilly Northumbria, and have seen one fly in a little wearily over the Northumbrian coast after its long overseas migration in spring. The pied flycatcher nests in holes in trees, and lays its eggs of unspotted blue late in the month of May. The song of this attractive bird is a softly whistled phrase—a friendly little song, rather like the blackbird's song, but softer.

The *crossbill* is a bird which haunts coniferous woods. In Britain two species of crossbill are recognised—the common crossbill and the Scottish crossbill. The Scottish crossbill is rather the larger of the two, and the bill is more massive. This bird is a resident in the ancient pine forests of the highlands, but the common crossbill nests chiefly in England and its numbers are increased by great periodical immigrations in late summer and early autumn from the Continent.

The crossbill can be identified by its bill, the mandibles at the tips being crossed. In more than one country there is a legend to account for the crossed bill and the red plumage of the crossbill. The legend is that the bird used its utmost strength to withdraw the nails which held Christ to the cross. But the nails were driven in too firmly, and the bird, with mangled bill and with plumage dyed with Christ's blood, was forced by exhaustion to desist from its good work. As a mark of honour the crossbill's plumage (in the male) remains red,

21 A Sparrow Hawk and her Family

22 A Hawfinch feeding her Young

23 A Greater Spotted Woodpecker

24 A Male Green Woodpecker

and the bill crossed, to this day. The crossbill is one of the earliest British birds to nest, and eggs are sometimes laid in January and February.

The *siskin*, a small bird with lovely green plumage, yellow rump and eyestripe and black crown, haunts the same coniferous forests as the crossbill, but its nest is usually in the high branches of the trees. It is more numerous in Scotland than in England.

The *lesser redpoll*, a small bird with a dark crimson crown and characteristic undulating flight, while flying utters its call-note continuously, and seems to travel frequently from place to place, even during the nesting season, when it may be heard passing high over woods and valleys. Its nest is neat and small; its eggs are blue, spotted with brown.

Hawfinches are birds partly of the garden, partly of the woodland. These birds can be recognised by the strong, heavy bill, the stout head, the short tail, and the white wing patch. Their food consists of seeds and kernels of many kinds. In the garden their presence is sometimes detected by shredded pea-pods, or the split stones of cherries. Hawfinches are very local in their distribution, and are nowhere common.

Three species of *woodpecker* inhabit the woodlands of Britain—the green woodpecker or yaffle, the greater spotted woodpecker and the lesser spotted woodpecker.

The *green woodpecker's* laughing cry is heard often in England and Wales, but in Scotland the bird is rare, although in 1912 it nested in the Loch Lomond area. The green woodpecker's flight is rapid and undulating. The bird is found not only in woodlands but in open country where stately, solitary trees stand. The green woodpecker tunnels out its own nesting hole in the trunk of a tree, but is often driven away from the place by a pair of starlings, which have watched the excavations with envy.

The *greater spotted woodpecker*, with boldly pied plumage, crimson patch on the head and crimson under tail coverts, is a most handsome bird. This woodpecker is found nesting in England and Wales and also in Scotland. Its history in Scotland is interesting. Here it became extinct about the middle of the nineteenth century, but has now re-established itself in the ancient forests of birch and pine in the highlands. In these pine forests are old trees, long since dead; the bark has disappeared, and the greyish-white stems, smooth and strong, rise like skeletons in the forest. If these trunks be examined they will almost always be found to show old marks of boring by woodpeckers, and it is possible that these holes were made by greater spotted woodpeckers a hundred years ago, before the old race of birds disappeared from the highlands.

The *lesser spotted woodpecker* does not occur in Scotland, but in some districts of the south of England is numerous. It is a small bird, no larger than a chaffinch, and its plumage is barred rather than pied. All the woodpeckers lay white, glossy eggs.

The *waxwing*, a bird of the Arctic forests, is an irregular and sometimes a common visitor to our woods during the autumn and winter. Little is known of the cause of these periodic excursions across the sea to this country, but they occur usually during stormy weather from the east or north-east. The waxwing is a handsome bird. It has a conspicuous chestnut-brown crest, the tips of the tail feathers are lemon coloured, there is a white bar on the wings, and the chin is black. The secondary wing feathers are prolonged into red, shiny, waxy tips, and these give the bird its name. During the winter of 1936–7 an extensive immigration of waxwings occurred in Britain. These birds penetrated west to the Hebrides, and in Skye at least two were found dead and were sent to me. One of the birds was found lifeless and starved in the sitting-room of a house. It had perhaps entered through the open window in search of food, for trees and bushes are rare in the Isle of Skye, and the berries which form the waxwing's main food in winter are few and far between. Waxwings are tame birds; they have no experience of the domestic cat as an enemy, and in the Isle of Mull during this recent immigration a cat easily accounted for two of these wanderers.

No account of woodland birds would be complete without mention of the tribe of the *owls*, the farmer's friends. Of the wood owls there are three common species—the long-eared owl, the tawny or brown owl, and the little owl. The solemn human-like stare of the owls makes us feel friendly towards them. They are indeed our friends, for they capture innumerable mice, rats and voles. Even the little owl (which is not a true British owl, but which was introduced into this country by Mr. Meade-Waldo in 1874 and by Lord Lilford about the year 1886), has now been cleared by a scientific enquiry of certain charges laid against it.

The *long-eared owl* is distinguished by the long ear-like tufts on its head. It is smaller than the tawny owl, and is truly nocturnal, being seldom seen by day. A friend of mine in the early winter of 1937, when out shooting in the Isle of Skye, happened to come upon a family of eight long-eared owls roosting in a small tree. The owls showed little fear, and he actually was able to catch one. The *tawny owl* is a larger bird, and its hooting in the woods at night is a pleasant thing to hear. I have sometimes succeeded in imitating a tawny owl sufficiently well to draw a reply from the invisible bird. The long-eared owl nests usually in a disused squirrel's dray, in the deserted nest of a magpie or rook, or on the ground at the foot of a tree, but the tawny owl nests generally in a hollow tree and returns each year to the same nesting-place. It is sometimes fearless in the defence of its nest and will attack a man by knocking off his hat or even burying its talons in his scalp. The *snowy owl*, a rare wanderer from the far north, is sometimes seen in late autumn or in spring far up some highland glen, and its snowy plumage and majestic flight render it unforgettable.

Like the owls, the *woodcock* is partly nocturnal, and indeed, unless it is disturbed, is rarely seen flying abroad during the hours of full daylight. The woodcock is an early nester, and a favourite nesting site is in a dry bed of leaves and bracken beneath birch or beech trees. Four eggs are laid, and the owner sits very closely upon them, yet I have found that if she be forced to leave the nest and if the eggs be touched by the human hand, she will invariably desert them.

It seems now to be conceded that the woodcock does upon occasion carry her young when danger threatens them, but she more usually feigns injury and endeavours by flopping over the ground ahead of him to draw the intruder away from her family.

Many of the British woodcock fly south to Ireland, and some to France and Spain, at the coming of wintry weather: their places are taken by a great immigration from Scandinavia and North Russia.

During the spring and early summer months the woodcock at sunset leaves its woody retreats and flies with curious, erratic flight backwards and forwards above the tree-tops, uttering a grunting, and again a sharp hissing cry. This the Scandinavians call the "ròding" of the woodcock.

The *nightjar* is another nocturnal or crepuscular bird of the woodlands, and haunts also commons and wastes, where whins and bracken give cover. The love song of the nightjar is a reverberating "churring," unlike the notes of any other British bird.

There is an old belief that nightjars embody the souls of unbaptised infants doomed to wander for ever in the air. Gilbert White put it on record that "the country people have a notion that the nightjar is very injurious to weanling calves, by inflicting, as it strikes at them, the fatal distemper known to cow-leeches by the name of puckerage." Puckerage is still one of the local names of the nightjar. Another name is goat-sucker, from the tale which occurs in Aristotle, that the nightjar, "flying to the udders of she-goats, sucks them and thus gets its name: they say that the udder withers when it has sucked at it, and that the goat goes blind." A peculiarity of the nightjar is that it perches longitudinally on a bough, and not crosswise like other birds.

When spring has reached the moorlands, and the rough winds from the east are but a memory, it is pleasant to listen to the calling of *cuckoos* from the green mists of the forest.

> Sumer is icumen in,
> Lhude sing cuccu!
> Groweth sed, and bloweth med,
> And springth the wude nu——
> Sing cuccu!

Thus begins the "Cuckoo Song" of the thirteenth century, and down through the years poets have found inspiration in the voice of this wandering bird, which returns to Britain in April from its winter quarters in Africa. It is an unfortunate omen if the first cuckoo should be heard when the hearer has no money in his or her pocket, for on turning one's money at the first call of the cuckoo the increase of that money is assured. In Yorkshire it is a custom for children to sing round a cherry-tree:

> Cuckoo, cherry-tree,
> Come down and tell me
> How many years afore I dee.

Each child then shakes the tree in turn, and counts the number of the petals which have fallen to the ground. These stand for the years of the child's life. There is a curious old belief that the cuckoo in winter is changed into a sparrow hawk.

A female cuckoo is believed to lay up to twenty-six eggs in one season. These are laid in the nests of many species of birds,

25 A Lesser Spotted Woodpecker at the Nesting Hole

26 A Tawny Owl with prey

27 A Young Tawny Owl

and when the nest is in a site where the cuckoo cannot sit upon it, she lays her egg outside and, lifting it in her bill, places it in the nest.[1] Although many species of birds are victimised, an individual cuckoo will usually lay in the nests of the same species; thus a cuckoo which lays her first egg in a meadow pipit's nest will probably lay her dozen and more eggs in other meadow pipits' nests, and a cuckoo which lays her first egg in a reed warbler's nest will go on laying in reed warblers' nests. The cuckoo lays a very small egg for the size of the bird, and the egg hatches out with remarkable speed—in about twelve days. The young cuckoo very soon after it is hatched heaves the rightful inmates of the nest out over the edge by burrowing under them, lifting them on its back—specially hollowed for that purpose—and then throwing them out into the cold, inhospitable world, where they do not long survive. It is remarkable that the parents of these ejected babies should pay no heed to them and should allow them to die while lavishing all their affection on their large foster-child.

The *sparrow hawk*, with which the cuckoo is sometimes confused (though indeed the flight of the cuckoo is slow and laboured when compared with the quick movements of the sparrow hawk) is found in most British woodlands. Many people are unable to differentiate between sparrow hawk and kestrel when the two are in full flight, but the sparrow hawk's wings are broad and rounded while the wings of the kestrel are the wings of a true falcon opposed to a hawk—they are clear-cut and sharply pointed. The sparrow hawk's prey is chiefly small and medium-sized birds, taken on the wing, but it has been known to snatch a full-grown lapwing from its nest, and to kill woodpigeon, teal and moorhen, and its own double, the cuckoo!

A delightful little falcon of the woodlands is the *hobby*. Its flight is the perfection of grace, and the long sickle-shaped wings and short tail make it when seen in the summer air not unlike a giant swift. The hobby is a summer resident in England, and in Scotland is almost unknown. It is one of the latest birds in England to nest, and eggs are rarely seen before the second week in June. The hobby hunts and captures the fastest of birds and even dragon-flies. Its prey is often the swallow and martin, and sometimes even the swift. It is very uncommon in most districts.

The *kite* formerly bred in the Scottish highlands, but has now been exterminated everywhere except in Wales where, thanks

[1] A book containing much original and valuable information is "The Truth about the Cuckoo" by Edgar Chance.

to the efforts of certain public-spirited landowners and to the Royal Society for the Protection of Birds, a few—a very few—pairs still nest, under the closest protection. The long pointed wings and the deeply cleft tail cause the kite to be unmistakable on the wing. Is it too much to hope that this fine bird may one day nest again in the pine forests of the central highlands, where an old nest of the species—forty or fifty years old, if not more—remained until recently in the fork of the pine-tree where it was built?

And now the mustering rooks innumerable
Together sail and soar.

Throughout Britain, wherever there are trees, the *rook* makes its home. It is a wise bird, and many instances are on record of rooks deserting a tree of the rookery when that tree was apparently sound, yet its subsequent fall showed that the birds had more knowledge of their home than the human owner of the tree. There is, too, a belief in many parts of this country that when rooks for no apparent reason desert a rookery the death of the heir to the estate, or the downfall of the family, is at hand. Many rooks frequent their rookery not only during the nesting season but throughout the winter. Each winter dawn they set out on the flight to the feeding grounds. This flight may be a dozen miles and more, and in the treeless district of the north of Skye rooks each morning in winter may be seen winging their way overhead and at dusk returning high over the sea towards distant unseen trees. The rook's greyish-white face distinguishes it from the carrion crow, a bird that is most destructive to eggs and young birds. The rook's bill is bare at the base: the bill of the carrion crow is feathered. Carrion crows each year breed, or attempt to breed, in the parks of London, but they are not encouraged here, because of the numbers of young ducklings which they kill. Another point of difference between crow and rook is the appearance of the plumage. In the carrion crow the feathers in repose are held close to the body: in the rook the feathers of the flanks hang loosely over the thighs.

The *magpie* holds its own except in East Anglia, despite the fact that every gamekeeper's gun is against it, and the dome-shaped nest, built sometimes in hedges, sometimes in trees, may be seen throughout the British Isles. There is an old saying of the magpie that

28 A Jay with her Young

29 A Young Cuckoo being fed by a Pied Wagtail

30 A Nightjar approaching her Eggs

31 A Nuthatch at the Nesting Hole

32 A Rookery in Spring

One's mirth, two's grief,
Three's a wedding, four's death,
Five's heaven, six is hell,
Seven's the deil's ain sel'.

The *jay*, too, is able to take care of itself, and although an arrant thief of the eggs of other birds, and shot without mercy by game preservers, is holding its own and is extending its range towards the north.

A typical woodland bird is the *wood pigeon*, but in the Orkney Islands there is at least one wood pigeon colony on a treeless hillside, on which the birds nest in long heather. Enormous numbers of immigrant wood pigeons cross the North Sea to Britain each autumn and are very destructive to the crops in East Anglia. The beautiful *turtle-dove* nests in England, and although it does not nest in Scotland it is sometimes seen in that country on migration. During recent years I have seen two turtle-doves in the Hebrides in the early autumn. One of the birds was on the treeless island of Coll, the other was in the north of the Isle of Skye. In both instances the dove was very tame.

This chapter on woodland birds will be concluded by a very brief account of two game birds—the *capercaillie* and the *pheasant*. Both species are of a race alien to Britain. The nearest home of the pheasant is the Caucasus. There the pheasant pairs in the ordinary way, but in Britain it has formed less admirable habits and is now polygamous—each cock takes a number of wives.

The *capercaillie* is largest of all British game birds, and as it flies through the pine forests which are its home it looks sometimes like a gigantic blackcock. The original capercaillie of the Scottish highlands became extinct about the year 1760. The species was re-introduced from Sweden into Perthshire in the early years of the nineteenth century, and has since then flourished and spread. The cock caper is a magnificent bird, and flies with great power: the hen sits close upon the nest, but when disturbed becomes very wary.

During a phase of his courtship display the male capercaillie is oblivious to danger, and in Scandinavia and other continental countries he is stalked and shot by hunters at this time. Much skill is necessary to approach the male capercaillie during his display, for the hen birds warn him of the approach of danger.

CHAPTER III

Birds of the Field or Common

BENEATH the blue sky of summer, in which white, billowy clouds idly drift, the commons—waste lands they are sometimes erroneously called—and fields of Britain are the home of many birds. These birds do not shun the brilliance of the sunlight, as do some of the woodland birds; they are happy beneath a cloudless sky, with no more shade than a tussock of grass or a frond of swaying bracken. Supreme among these birds of the open spaces in the joyousness of its song is the *skylark.*

Hail to thee, blithe spirit!
Bird thou never wert,
That from heaven or near it
Pourest thy full heart
In profuse strains of unpremeditated art.

Higher still and higher
From the cloud thou springest,
Like a cloud of fire:
The blue deep thou wingest,
And singing still dost soar, and soaring
ever singest.

In certain parts of Scotland the lark is supposed to sing:

Up in the lift we go,
Tehee, tehee, tehee, tehee!
There's not a shoemaker on the earth
Can make a shoe to me, to me!
Why so, why so, why so?
Because my heel is as long as my toe.

The reference in the last line is to the lark's long hind claw.

In the Hebrides the skylark is often known as *Fosgag Mhuire*, the Virgin Mary's Linnet, and above the green, grassy lands of the Outer Hebrides, where the deep blue of the Atlantic ends in a snow-white strand, the skylark's song is heard from dawn until, at ten o'clock in the evening, the sun sinks, glowing and quivering, beneath the sea. The skylark when singing seems full

33 A Whitethroat with her Young

34 A Skylark with her Young

35 A Cock Stonechat with his Family

to overflowing with rapture and with the pure joy of life. He is heedless of the effort it costs him—as cost him it must—to pour forth his song without ceasing while climbing almost vertically heavenwards, for it must be remembered that the lark uses his wings incessantly to drive him up and does not, like the eagle, climb on motionless wings, without effort.

The skylark sings chiefly in the air, but at times makes music on the ground also. At night the singer finds shelter in a tussock of grass, and may spread his wings with startling suddenness at your feet and be off.

The *corn bunting* has a slight resemblance to a robust blunt-headed skylark, lacking white outer tail feathers, but in character it is very different from the lark. The skylark is brimful of energy; the corn bunting is a lazy bird, so lazy indeed that when it does rather reluctantly take a short flight—it rarely makes more than a short flight—it still holds its legs hanging earthward in a thoroughly untidy and slipshod manner. It would often be overlooked were it not for the strange, wheezy little song which the male sings, his favourite singing station being a telegraph wire. The corn bunting makes her nest in hay- or corn-fields, and, in order no doubt to find as much cover as possible, is a late nester. The eggs are rarely laid until June, and as two broods are reared in the summer the second brood may be still in the nest in August or even September. This bird is extremely clever in misleading the human searcher after its nest, and to watch a pair of corn buntings carrying insect life for their young is to realise how careful they are to hoodwink the human observer. The corn bunting nests in suitable places throughout the British Isles, but is decreasing in most districts. It is believed to be polygamous.

The *cirl bunting*, another frequenter of open spaces, resembles the yellow hammer, but the male may be distinguished from that bird by the black throat and ear coverts and the olive-grey band on the breast. It is a local bird, and is not found in Scotland.

A more numerous bird by far is the *meadow pipit*, a bird which closely resembles its relative the tree pipit, but is rather smaller. Like the tree pipit, the meadow pipit loves to fly up almost perpendicularly into the air, and having reached a considerable height, to soar earthward, with upturned tail acting as rudder. During the upward flight and again during the earthward soaring a pleasant little song is sung, but that uttered on the upward flight is quite distinct from that heard on the downward. Whereas the tree pipit "takes off" from a tree, the meadow pipit begins its song-flight from a wall, or boulder, or from the ground. Meadow pipits may be seen often in hot chase of a cuckoo, which perhaps they take for a hawk, and their distrust for the cuckoo is well founded, for no bird is so frequently victimised as the meadow pipit. Most British meadow pipits migrate south and south-west at the end of the summer. In September 1937 I met with a party of these birds on the rocky summit of Sgurr na Banachdich, one of the Cuillin hills of Skye. The pipits rose into the mist, and sailed daintily and carelessly over a great 1,000-feet precipice.

The *linnet* is a characteristic bird on most commons and whin thickets. The male, with handsome crimson feathers on his forehead and breast, in spring and early summer often perches on a whin bush, and sings his twittering warble of a song, and at times, after the manner of the meadow pipit, flies a little way into the air and descends, singing, with outspread tail.

Whitethroats are summer visitors. They are rather shy birds, and would often be undetected were it not for the song. Both the common whitethroat and the lesser whitethroat are British-nesting birds. The common whitethroat nests in Scotland as well as in England, but the lesser whitethroat is a rare bird north of the Tweed. The song of the common whitethroat is a curious medley of sound, with whistling mellow notes and again with harsh guttural gratings and chucklings. The lesser whitethroat's song is very different, and is indeed very like the cirl bunting's song. The lesser whitethroat is rather smaller than the common whitethroat, but the chief distinction is the absence of the reddish edges to the secondary wing feathers which are noticeable in the common whitethroat.

The *stonechat* and the *whinchat* frequent the same ground in summer, but in winter their homes are very far apart. The stonechat is a confirmed stay-at-home, and summer and winter its perky figure may be seen on the same ground. But when summer goes, the whinchat flies south, and on the winter morning when the stonechat is surveying its native heath the whinchat is catching insects beneath the unclouded blue of the African sky. It is curious how many British birds have received names which are absurd, or at all events thoroughly inapt. The oyster catcher is one; the stonechat is another.

The stonechat is rarely seen in stony places, for it prefers bracken or gorse-covered slopes; it is probable that those who originally gave it the name confused it with the wheatear: another theory is that the name was given this bird because of its alarm note, which might be likened to two stones being knocked together. The male stonechat is a handsome bird, and his black head, broad white collar and prominent white wing-patch make him a conspicuous object as he flies restlessly about the whins, the while uttering his fussy and determined alarm note, which sounds rather like "hweet-chat, hweet-chat." Stonechats are early nesters, and some of them have laid before the first whinchat has arrived from its winter quarters overseas. The nest is skilfully concealed, and the birds are adepts at misleading the person who is in search of it. The small eggs are bluish-green, with usually a band of fine rusty specks at the larger end. Two broods, or perhaps even three, are reared in a season. In severe winter weather those stonechats which live on the coast sometimes feed on the sands along with true shore birds such as the dunlin and the redshank. I have watched, in frosty weather, a cock stonechat perch on a post on wet sands near full tide, and have seen him fly time after time down to the sand as a wave recedes, and pick up apparently one of the small sandhoppers left stranded. On seaside golf courses in frosty weather a pair of stonechats sometimes attach themselves to the greenkeeper who is re-turfing a putting green, and become so tame that they perch upon his barrow or even on his spade. Whinchats, perhaps because they have seen more of the world, are less confiding. The whinchat is a more slender and less sturdy bird, and the male has less bold colouring than the male stonechat, and can be distinguished from him by the prominent white eye-stripe. In Scotland, and even in the Hebrides, both whinchat and stonechat are found, and add character to many a lonely acre of grazing land where they share their domain with the wheatear.

The *wheatear* deserves special mention because it is, with the possible exception of the chiffchaff, our earliest summer visitor. The males are almost always the first to arrive. As you walk, one day of late March, over the rough pasture lands beloved of the species you may be thinking to yourself that spring is still far off. The coarse grass is still brown and withered; the wind is harsh and warns of an approaching snow squall; no film of green shows even on the banks of short-cropped grass leaning to the south. When a small bird jauntily rises from the sheltered side of a stone wall and flies a short distance away, his white rump conspicuous as he flies, you are therefore taken by surprise. This bird of pale greys and buffs and black and white has flown far, and surely after his winter quarters in tropical Africa he finds the British March air a little cold, and food a little scarce. Snow may return and cover the ground after the wheatears come, and rarely a spring passes but these birds must go through lean times before winter has at last receded towards the north.

The wheatear, besides being almost the first migrant to reach us in spring, is perhaps the last to leave us in autumn; indeed, I have sometimes seen the species in this country in November. The song, which is sweet and well modulated, is often uttered on the wing. The nest is made down a rabbit hole, under a stone, or in a hole in a stone wall. I have known of a nest in a small hole in the wall of an inhabited house in the Isle of Skye. The eggs are pale blue, and are usually unmarked.

The *pied wagtail* sometimes shares the same wall as the wheatear, and its dainty flight, and delicate, hurrying walk as it chases an insect, are characteristic of all wagtails. The pied wagtail is not so wide a traveller as the wheatear, but may leave Britain at the close of summer, and nestlings ringed in England have been found in France and in Portugal.

There is an old Border belief that the wagtail should wag its tail nine times on alighting, before it begins to run about or feed. If the tail is wagged less than nine times, or more than nine times, it is unlucky for the person who is counting.

Pied wagtails in winter sometimes choose unexpected roosting-places. There is a small tree in Dublin where each night throughout the winter hundreds of the species roost, in the full glare of the street lamps, and this instance of city roosting is not unique.

Of the *Dartford warbler* and the *grasshopper warbler* I can say nothing, for it has not been my good fortune to know these birds, but W. H. Hudson in one of his books gives, in his own inimitable style, an arresting description of the home life of the Dartford warbler. Nor have I had the good fortune to hear the song of the wood lark which is said on occasion to last a full half-hour as the bird swings in wide circles above its sitting mate. The ascent in the song flight of the wood lark is made not vertically as the skylark makes it, but in a spiral curve.

36 A Whinchat on a bracken frond

37 A Cock Wheatear

38 A Corncrake with her Eggs

In England the wood lark is a resident, but is nowhere common, although it is most numerous in the southern counties. In Scotland it regularly arrives on Fair Isle in October and sometimes remains throughout the winter.

Of the larger birds of field and common one of the most characteristic is the *lapwing* or peewit, or green plover. It is February when the lapwings begin to arrive at their inland nesting-places. Many of the British lapwings have passed the winter in North Africa; others have travelled less far towards the south, but almost all of them have been away from Britain during the heart of winter. The British Isles, it is true, hold a large winter population of lapwings, but these birds are chiefly migrants from Scandinavian and Baltic countries. It was during the cold December of 1927 that the historic east to west crossing of the Atlantic was made by a great flock of lapwings. During the last week of the year, with an easterly gale and frost, these green plovers rose into the frosty air somewhere in the north of England, meaning, no doubt, to fly west to Ireland. But the storm was so severe that the birds failed to find Ireland and continued their flight west until they had reached Newfoundland. During their long ocean flight most unusual conditions prevailed over the whole of the Atlantic on their course. The wind that day averaged the high velocity of fifty-five miles an hour from the east at 1,000 feet above sea-level all the way across the ocean until approximately 200 miles from the Newfoundland coast, when it dropped light. Mr. H. F. Witherby gives a very interesting article in Vol. XXII of *British Birds* on this unique flight and reckons that, assuming the flying speed of a lapwing to be forty-five miles an hour, the crossing from England would have taken the birds twenty-four hours. One of these lapwings—many perished in the severe weather which set in shortly after they reached Newfoundland—bore a "British Birds" ring, placed on its leg in the Lake District in Cumberland in May of the previous year.

I have sometimes thought it curious that the lapwings should arrive in the upland districts of Scotland and England before the season of frost and snow has ended. In March their haunts may be snow- and frost-bound, and when this happens many lapwings die of starvation. The love of home must be great to cause them to leave the warmth of their winter quarters for the bleakness of snowy uplands in February. It is interesting that the lapwings which nest in the Hebrides should arrive almost a month later than those of the mainland. As the risk of snow and frost in the Hebrides is slight this late arrival is curious. A pertinent suggestion is that the Hebridean lapwings may winter in a different district, or even country, from those nesting on the mainland.

It is my experience that on the mainland of England and Scotland the lapwing begins his love flight and song during the first days of March. Backwards and forwards the male lapwing flies with mad, swerving flight, the broad, rounded, creaking wings being driven fast. He then rises a little way almost vertically into the air, seems to turn a back somersault, and throws to the March wind his loud, defiant love song which sounds something like "whey willuch ou weep, willuch ou willuch ehyuweeep." His mate is perhaps standing, apparently heedless and unresponsive, on the ground beneath him, but she may now rise, and together they perform an intricate love dance in the air. On suitable ground, the love songs of several lapwings may be heard at the same time: they are heard most loudly, I think, before rain.

The lapwing lays early in April, but I have seen eggs as late as June. Four eggs are laid, thickly blotched with black; on one or two occasions I have seen five in a nest. The sitting bird is careful not to betray the nest, and she usually runs furtively a little distance over the ground before swinging up into the air. Was it not Chaucer who wrote of her as "the false Lapwing, full of treachery"? After the young are hatched—and they leave the nest, running actively, the first day of their lives—the parents show great anxiety on their behalf when danger threatens. They will swoop repeatedly at a dog, and will fly low over the head of a man, calling angrily: the young crouch motionless on the ground until the danger is past. The male lapwing is ever on the watch for bird enemies—and he thinks every bird *is* an enemy—passing overhead. When he sees them approach he mounts quickly into the air and dashes at his utmost speed to the attack. Having escorted or driven the presumed enemy, be it crow, rook, or seagull, off his beat, the lapwing flies back and again settles on the ground. When gulls or rooks are numerous his life is one continual round of alarms, and all his efforts may not save his chick from a hungry seagull. There is no bird that a lapwing will not venture to attack, and I once saw him pursuing a heedless golden eagle.

Lapwings are unfitted to withstand prolonged frost, and many

39 A Lapwing at the Nest

40 A Barn Owl caught by flashlight at the Nesting Hole

succumb during a severe winter. They then haunt the fields bordering the coast, and sometimes descend at low tide to the shore itself, and feed on low seaweed-covered rocks, but they seem to have difficulty in finding sufficient food on the shore.

A thorn in the lapwing's flesh during the winter months is the black-headed gull. The gull stands near a feeding lapwing and waits until that bird has dragged a worm from the ground. Its eye is keen, and even if the lapwing be a hundred yards away from it, the gull notices at once the capture of the worm and flies to the attack. Backwards and forwards the gull chases the plover, until the lapwing is obliged to drop its prize, which is at once swallowed by the gull. Both black-headed and common gulls habitually play this—for them—satisfying game.

The *corncrake* or land rail is a summer visitor to Britain and is dependent for cover on growing grass and corn in the fields. It reaches us early in May, and its harsh music is heard throughout the short nights of early summer. The corncrake would seem to be a ventriloquist, and his voice comes now from one direction, now from another. There are certain curious legends concerning the corncrake. A French name for it is *roy de cailles*, the king of the quails, from an old belief that before migration the quails chose a corncrake to lead them on their great adventure. It seems to have been thought in England that the corncrake in winter changed into a water rail, and resumed its own form again the following spring.

When the corncrake first arrives at its summer haunts the cover of growing grass and corn, in a backward spring, is insufficient for it, and then it may be seen as a surprisingly small brown bird furtively running through the short grass. Through the day the bird is silent, but when evening comes its "crek, crek" rises, with the evening mist, from the meadows. Despite its large clutch of eggs—which on occasion may number eighteen—the corncrake in most districts is decreasing. One suggestion to account for this decrease is that the horse-drawn and motor-propelled reapers move so swiftly that they give the sitting corncrake little opportunity to leave her nest before being cut down, and indeed in the Hebrides, where the scythe is still used, the bird seems to be holding its own.

The *stone curlew*, called by eighteenth-century writers the thick-kneed bustard, is a summer resident in the downlands of England. In appearance it is a large bullet-headed plover with prominent yellow eyes. It runs fast, with short steps, or flies swiftly just above the ground with its long yellow legs outstretched. Its note is a wailing cry, resembling the curlew's call. It is a summer visitor, and winters in the countries bordering on the Mediterranean and in Africa.

The calling of the *partridge* is inseparable from the commons and fields of Britain. The male partridge's cry is a loud and hoarse "caer-wit, *caer*-wit," a cry which in quiet weather is heard at a considerable distance. The hen partridge sits very closely on the nest, so closely indeed that she is sometimes decapitated by a scythe or reaper. When I was a boy I saw a partridge meet its death in a remarkable way. It was an autumn afternoon, with a strong south wind blowing, and a covey of partridges flew at express speed down wind over the road along which I was cycling. One of the birds struck a telegraph wire: the head dropped at my feet, but the body, because of its weight and momentum, continued perhaps twenty or thirty yards in the air before thudding to earth.

It is curious that the *partridge* has become extinct in the Isle of Skye within living memory. A friend of mine tells me that he remembers fifty brace of partridges being shot on his ground in a season: now there is not a single partridge in the whole island. He explains the disappearance of the birds by the change in the agricultural conditions in the island. In his youth the island was farmed by large farmers. These have now given way to the crofter, and the crofter, having only small fields, and keeping dogs and cats, has made the place unsuitable for partridges. It is perhaps a point in support of this theory that lapwings do not nest in the fields in Skye, but on the rough moor pasture.

The red-legged partridge, rather larger than the common partridge and distinguished by its bright red legs, was introduced from abroad into Suffolk about the year 1770. Subsequent importations have been made, and the bird is now found in many districts of England.

> Alone and warming his five wits
> The white owl on the belfry sits.

The *barn owl* spends the day in clefts in cliffs, hollow trees, and old ruins. In dull weather it sometimes sallies forth to its hunting before sunset, and when seen in daylight this owl's white face and underparts are unmistakable.

The shriek of the barn owl when heard in the dusk of a

summer midnight is strange and unearthly: a barn owl made its home in a cranny of a sea cliff near my home in the north of Skye, and not knowing it was there, my wife and I for some time were at a loss to understand the high shriek which from time to time—at intervals of several weeks—broke the silence of the northern dusk. The barn owl should be protected, for it preys chiefly on rats and mice and, as I have said, may begin its good work before daylight has waned.

This chapter would not be complete without a brief account of two winter migrants to commons and fields—the *fieldfare* and the *redwing*. The fieldfare is like a large thrush, but its grey neck and rump are distinctive. It is a shy bird, and is difficult to approach. In the birch woods of northern Norway I have seen fieldfare and redwing nesting together, and it is curious that at the nesting haunts the fieldfare should be much bolder than the redwing, because at their British winter quarters the redwing is much tamer than the fieldfare. The redwing, a delicate bird in size similar to the song thrush, can be recognised by the white stripe above the eye and the chestnut-red flanks. This bird is a passage migrant and winter visitor to Britain, and it is believed that two forms exist—the Iceland redwing and the Scandinavian redwing—and that each visits the British Isles in winter. In the Isle of Skye, where most of my redwing observations have been made, the redwing is a winter and spring visitor, and is most numerous in late March and April. During these months our small lawn is sometimes full of redwings, feeding like thrushes on the worms, and the birds perch on the garden wall—we have no trees in our district—and practise their song, which they will utter in its full beauty a few weeks later in Scandinavian birch forests.

A few days ago I came upon a redwing with a broken wing. A wire fence was close to it, and it appeared that the bird, flying low on migration during the night hours, had struck one of the wires. The injured redwing ran quickly over the rough grass, but its power of flight had gone; and I could not but regret its plight and that after a long overseas flight, accomplished in safety, it should have met this disaster on a low fence hundreds of miles from the land of its birth.

Perhaps this chapter should end with a few words on the *shrikes*, strikingly coloured birds with strong bills. The great grey shrike on migration visits the east coast of Britain, but the red-backed shrike is the only member of the family which nests with us. Shrikes have the curious habit of impaling their prey on a "larder," which is usually a spike on some hedgerow thorn. They prey upon insects, and also on small birds and their young.

41 A Grey Wagtail feeding her Young

42 A Goldfinch at the Nest

43 A Raven croaking in full flight

CHAPTER IV

Birds of the Moors, Glens and Lesser Hills

MOORLAND birds are usually strong and independent. They live in open spaces where in summer there is no shelter from the fierce rays of the sun and in winter the winds of storm and drifting snow sweep with unbridled fury over the face of the land. Certain of these birds find it impossible to obtain food at their nesting haunts during the winter months: some of them fly to the coast; others leave Britain for more genial lands to the south.

The *curlew* is the spirit of the moors. The song of these birds—both male and female sing—is one of the most lovely songs in nature. It is curious that no poet seems to have noticed the curlew's song. I do not think Keats wrote of it, nor Shelley, nor indeed any of the great poets. But to some lovers of nature the curlew's song means more than the rapturous music of the nightingale, for it breathes out the soul of the lonely places where the mists drift low and the streams after rain sing a loud, imperious song. Long ago the curlew was considered an uncanny bird, partly because of its strange-looking bill of inordinate length, and partly because of its harsh shriek, uttered when the bird is suddenly disturbed or when its young are in danger.

It is mid-March when curlews return to the moors from their winter quarters—perhaps from Ireland, perhaps from Spain, Portugal or even Africa. The bird lover always records in the mind with singular pleasure that first day in spring when the curlew is seen and heard on the moors. Flying at no great height from the ground, the long-billed singer mounts a little way into the air on tremulous wings, then glides downward, beginning, but not continuing, the song. This "song trial" is repeated several times and at last the singer seems to say to itself, "Now for it," and as it glides earthward a torrent of liquid music is released. Faster and ever faster and more rapturous grows the song and then, just as the singer is about to alight, the music ends with a long, mournful, wailing whistle which to the human ear conveys sadness and melancholy. But not all spring days inspire the curlew to song, and there are seasons when the birds one morning find that their moor is snowbound. Day succeeds day, and the frost each night strengthens so that the last of the feeding swamps are frozen over. Disaster then overtakes the clan of the curlew, and many succumb: their starved bodies are later found where, starving and unable to fly, they had crept to make one last effort to break with their long bills the frozen crust which formed that impenetrable barrier between them and their food.

The eggs of the curlew are four in number; they are beautiful eggs, blotched and spotted with dark brown on a ground of pale green. The young curlews are able to run actively on the day they are hatched, and when many pairs of curlews are guarding their young on a moor, the human walker who disturbs their privacy is deafened by a continuous wild shrieking of alarm notes, very different to the love songs which he has heard earlier in the season, and which he still hears at intervals.

The *red grouse* is an important bird, and brings much money into Britain. The grouse moors of this country give employment to many men, and to not a few landowners the red grouse is the chief source of livelihood. It is the only bird which we in Britain may claim to be our very own, for in a truly wild state it is found only in the British Isles. It is believed that the red grouse and the ptarmigan came from a common stock and when the ice age retreated and the lower moors were no longer habitually snowbound in winter, the red grouse ceased to grow a winter dress of white. It is well known among sportsmen that heavy shooting on a moor causes the grouse to become wild and unapproachable and to form early into packs, and that these packs in autumn may consist of hundreds of birds. A recent visit to a deer forest where grouse are scarcely disturbed has led me to think that this habit of collecting into large packs is artificial, and that the birds if undisturbed would remain in pairs throughout the summer and autumn. At all events the red grouse of this deer forest were still in pairs at the end of October and were as fearless as they would have been on a grouse moor in spring.

"Rub-a-dub-dub" cries the cock grouse and then "Go-back, go-back" as he rises from your feet with a whirring of robust wings and skims away over the heather. Indeed there is a quality of robustness in the male grouse in all his actions. He

44 A Curlew in flight

45 A Curlew and her Chick

46 Blackcock displaying

47 A Red Grouse brooding her Eggs

seems to be as strong as the boulders of his native moors, and is always, even in the hardest weather, full of cheeriness and self-confidence. Of recent years a sub-species of red grouse has been found to inhabit the British Isles. It is rather smaller, and more retiring, than the typical form, and has been named *lagopus scoticus hibernicus*. It is the grouse which inhabits the west of Ireland and the Outer Hebridean Islands.

The *black grouse*, of which the male is usually termed the blackcock and the female the greyhen, is a much scarcer bird than the red grouse and has decreased in many districts where formerly it was numerous. Thus in certain parts of the Isle of Mull the black grouse was found in considerable numbers until the year 1916, when the entire stock, with the exception of a few stragglers, disappeared; it was thought that the exceptional rains of October of that year had caused the birds to migrate in a body. In another Hebridean island—Raasay—where formerly good blackgame shooting was obtained, there is now scarcely a blackcock to be found, and in the Isle of Skye, too, the species at the present day is rarely seen.

Black grouse prefer moors on which a few Scots pines and birches grow. The species is remarkable because of the habit of the males—the blackcock—to meet each morning at dawn on some chosen knoll where the grass or heather is short (the same knoll is always frequented) and there to carry through a remarkable "display" which lasts from dawn to sunrise. This "display" is not a thing of the nesting season only, for I have watched it in the frosty dimness of a December morning. When it is yet so dark that it is difficult to see them, one blackcock after another flies up out of the dawn and alights on the knoll, and at once there is intense activity and excitement. The air becomes filled with low bubbling cries repeated quickly and eagerly as the blackcock challenge one another. Two birds approach one another in a crouching attitude. The wings are held slightly open and drooping; the head is almost touching the ground; the tail coverts are spread fanwise and the white inner tail coverts show up like snow in the uncertain light. Backwards and forwards the combatants delicately tread, their throats vibrating with their bubbling cries, and now and again they rush forward and, almost interlocked, rise a little way into the air, striking at one another with their feet, and uttering a high hissing note. No damage is usually done during these sparring bouts, but feathers are displaced and exceptionally blackcock have been found dead on the "displaying" ground where they had evidently been killed by a more serious fight than usual. When the sun rises and when his first golden rays light up the fighting ground of the blackcock, the birds fold their tail coverts, close their wings, cease their bubbling cries, assume their normal position, and feed in a friendly manner before flying off to begin the "daily round, the common task." One or two greyhens may be spectators of this early morning scene, but they are not always there, and the display and sparring seem at times to be the result of superfluous high spirits and ebullient energy. On a calm frosty morning of late winter or early spring the bubbling challenges of blackcock carry great distances in the quiet air and with the singing of the thrush and the trilling of the curlew form a happy symphony to greet the new day. The display is also seen in the evenings.

The redshank is known to all bird lovers: its larger relative, the *greenshank*, is a scarcer and more retiring bird, of much sagacity and nervousness. As its name implies, the greenshank's long legs are green and since those of the redshank are red, there is no difficulty in distinguishing one species from the other when the birds are seen at close quarters. The greenshank is a larger bird than the redshank and stands higher; it is also less approachable. It is a summer visitor to Britain, and its nesting-places are the lower moors of the Scottish highlands and, to a lesser extent, the islands. Greenshank arrive at their summer haunts early in April, and in May the nesting hollow is scraped out and the four handsome eggs are laid. It is at this time that the male greenshank sings his song, and surely among British singers he is a master in the quality and in the length of that song. The greenshank does not often sing, and the listener may frequent the bird's haunts for days without hearing the song. But when at length that song is heard it will scarcely be forgotten, for in it is a wild quality unique among British birds. Swinging in wide circles in the sky, so high as to be a mere speck in the heavens, the greenshank may for the space of half an hour repeat without pause his impetuous, almost breathless, fluting song. "Teuchi teuchi, clever clever: teuchi teuchi, clever clever"—these words may be set down as having a faint resemblance to the notes of the greenshank's song: the quality of the music is strangely wild, and all the time the bird is singing he is circling with undulating flight at his topmost speed. With slight pauses at intervals he may continue circling for an hour or more. The wing-beats are slower during these flights.

When concealed in a hide set up near a greenshank's nest I was once fortunate enough to be a witness of the "change-over" between the cock bird and the hen. The female was brooding at the time, and the male flew up and alighted on a stunted pine tree that grew in the boggy ground a few yards from the nesting site. The male greenshank after standing on this little tree and calling for some time flew down to the ground and very slowly walked towards the nest, all the time calling with a strong and low-toned musical whistle. The hen, crouching on the eggs, answered him with husky little cries, very subdued in volume, so as to avoid drawing the attention of possible enemies to her nest. Bowing and pausing, the male greenshank approached. He was evidently suspicious of the hide, and although I knew that he wished to relieve his mate on the eggs, I feared that his mistrust for the hide would cause him to retreat. With one eye glued to the small peephole at the front of the hide I watched, scarcely daring to breathe, his hesitating approach. Then, so quickly that my eye could not follow it, the "change-over" occurred—the male bird was sitting on the eggs, and the female had flown noiselessly away. It was only when I returned home and developed the plate which I had hurriedly exposed that I found I had been so fortunate as to obtain a clear record of the interesting event. The male greenshank in the photograph is seen standing over the eggs, and the female is in the act of rising to allow him to take her place.

It is unfortunate for the greenshank that its rarity and the beauty of its eggs have caused these eggs to be greatly prized by the egg collector, who offers large bribes for their discovery. Greenshank love to frequent the shores of some highland loch, in which they wade thigh-deep as they probe the mud and water weeds with their sensitive bills. When they rise into the air their deeper-toned whistle, larger size, and white rump at once distinguish them from the redshank.

I have seen greenshank and *golden plover* nesting on the same ground, but the golden plover generally prefers more open moors. This swift-winged plover nests on moors and grass-lands in suitable localities throughout Britain. It arrives early, sometimes in February, in flocks on the moors where later it will nest and, like the curlew, is occasionally caught by a recurrence of winter with disastrous results. A separate sub-species of golden plover—the northern golden plover—passes along the coasts of Britain on spring migration. This sub-species has more black on the plumage than the British golden plover, and is an extremely handsome bird. I believe that the golden plover which nest sparingly on the Cairngorm tablelands 3,000 feet above sea-level may be of this form.

Like the greenshank, the golden plover has an aerial song, and during this song the normal swift flight of the species is changed to a series of slow, owl-like, wing-beats: it is interesting that the down wing-thrust should then coincide with one note of the song and the upward beat with another. There is to my mind no doubt that the golden plover alters his flight in order that he may the more easily utter the two long whistled notes of which his song is composed. The oyster catcher, too, alters his usual rapid flight to slow wing-thrusts when singing on the wing.

Three *falcons* inhabit the moors and glens—the proud peregrine falcon, the merlin of swift flight, and the dainty hovering kestrel. All these birds are true falcons, with the dark and proud falcon eye. The *peregrine* is one of the swiftest British birds of the air: on its narrow, clean-cut wings it glides rather than flies at deceptive speed; it also upon occasion sails leisurely in spirals high in the air like eagle and buzzard. Peregrines prey largely upon ducks, and that even the male peregrine—a considerably smaller bird than the female—will not hesitate to attack a passing gaggle of geese was brought home to me one stormy day of early winter in the Isle of Skye. I was walking beneath a sea cliff, and saw a male peregrine perched on a buttress at the top of the rock. He suddenly flew out into the gale and when I looked up I saw that he had noticed the approach of a gaggle of grey geese fighting their way into the storm. Immediately over my head the peregrine made a stoop at one of the geese but, perhaps owing to the strength of the wind, he missed his mark, and the alarmed geese scattered with loud cries of alarm and flew out over the turbulent sea towards a distant island.

The peregrine falcon sometimes stoops at small birds, and only a few days ago I was the witness of a stern chase in mid-air. I happened to be standing outside our house, and high in the gloomy sky above my head noticed a falcon attacking a little bird. Backwards and forwards, up and down, the two flew,

48 A Greenshank on her Nest

49 A Golden Plover

50 A Female Kestrel holding a Field Vole

and I saw that the quarry was a lark and the pursuer a male peregrine falcon. After a time the lark was obviously tiring, and as the two hovered with quickly driven wings very close to one another I thought every moment the peregrine would snatch the lark and fly off with it. But this it was beyond its power to do, and the lark at last dived close to the house, and the peregrine, for the first time seeing me standing below him, flew rather defiantly and leisurely away, as though to show that he had little fear of me. As he flew, a flock of starlings rose beneath him and at them he made a half-hearted stoop before disappearing from my view. Birds of prey seem to view the starling's flesh with disfavour, and rarely kill and eat this bird if other food is available.

There is perhaps no other bird that inspires so much fear as the peregrine falcon. Watch a peregrine move with swift gliding flight over an isle where thousands of puffins and other sea-fowl are nesting. The air, until the moment of his passing, is thronged with puffins, but when the peregrine appears the birds vanish as if hidden by a magician's cloak. Most of them alight on the sea and dive beneath the surface, for the peregrine rarely takes prey from the water. It is strange that the appearance of a greater black-backed gull will cause these same puffins comparatively little alarm, although the greater black-back is a more deadly enemy than the peregrine, and each summer disembowels, but does not always kill, scores of unfortunate puffins.

The peregrine falcon is a fierce slayer and makes raids on most species of birds. Grouse are often killed, but the falcon's favourite prey in my own experience is the carrier pigeon, and if a peregrine's eyrie is in the flight-line of these pigeons, scores, and even hundreds, are taken. I have indeed known of clubs which have been forced to desist from flying pigeons because of the number of birds killed by falcons. The peregrine is also fond of rock pigeons, and on our coasts may often be seen in stern chase of them. But the rock dove is a swift flier and often escapes by dashing into the sanctuary of a cave in the rocks. I once looked out of my window and saw, immediately beneath it, a blue pigeon standing on the garden path only a few feet from me. Looking up, I saw a large female peregrine "waiting" overhead. The pigeon on seeing me so near flew about a hundred yards, and took refuge in a ditch of a field. The falcon followed, and things would have become interesting had it not been for the interference of a pair of grey crows, which in their impudent way began to annoy and mob the falcon, so that at last she became disgusted and flew off.

When the peregrine falcon kills its prey in the air the force of the death-dealing blow is so terrific that the victim's head is often severed from its body. Some authorities believe that the peregrine strikes with the edge of the wing, others with the foot.

In a peregrine's eyrie on a ledge of rock two hundred feet above a hill loch I found the remains of a coot, and it says much for the weight-lifting capacity of the peregrine that it was able to carry so heavy a bird as the coot up from the loch to the cliff. At this eyrie I saw the remains of two teal ducks and, on another occasion, a lapwing. It is on record that in a peregrine falcon's eyrie on May Island in the Firth of Forth a grouse was found, although May Island is eight miles out to sea, and there is no grouse moor on the mainland coast nearer than the Lammermoors or Pentlands, or the Ochill Hills of Fife.

The falcon broods so closely on her eyrie—which is a shallow hollow scraped in the earth on a rock ledge and sometimes lined with the bones of victims of previous years—that a deer-stalker once caught a peregrine on the nest. Although I did not actually see this occurrence I can readily believe it, for on one occasion I could myself have taken a brooding peregrine falcon. The eyrie was in a little hollow on a steep grassy slope of an uninhabited Hebridean island. I made my way along a narrow horizontal track trodden by the stirks which were pastured on the land, and put my head in at the entrance to the hollow. Two feet from me I saw in the gloom the fiery eyes of the falcon burning like lamps. So long as my head was there she was unable to leave the nesting hollow, but the instant I withdrew it she passed like a rocket out into the open air where, high in the sky, she flew backwards and forwards, shrieking defiance and rage at me. It was interesting that later in the season an eider duck appropriated the peregrine's nesting ledge and laid her eggs in the nest.

The peregrine falcon has from time immemorial been used in falconry, and it was reckoned that the falcon (the female peregrine) was a match for a wild goose and the tiercel or male for partridges and smaller game. The female is, of course, considerably larger than the male.

The *merlin*, not unlike the peregrine in its behaviour, is the smallest British falcon, and the male is scarcely larger than a

51 A Merlin brooding Eggs in the old nest of a Hooded Crow

52 A Buzzard bringing prey to the Nest

53 A Female Hen Harrier with her Family

full-grown blackbird. The male merlin is slate-blue; the female in her colouring might be mistaken for a kestrel, but her flight is very different, for she moves with dashing speed close to the ground. The merlin nests usually in long heather, and when the nesting-site is approached by man the birds become agitated and fly backwards and forwards overhead uttering a chattering scream not unlike, but shriller than, the alarm cry of the falcon. Although the merlin is shot by all gamekeepers it is interesting to record that game birds or their young have very rarely been seen at a merlin's nest. This falcon preys chiefly on small birds. Meadow pipit, and skylark, twite and thrush, are habitually taken, and the merlin is swift enough to fly down and capture a swallow.

The *kestrel*, another small falcon, is shot almost everywhere, and yet the food of this bird is largely rats, mice and field voles, spiders and beetles. When hunting above a steep heathery or grassy face the kestrel is at its best when an uprising current of wind supports it. It then hangs for minutes in the same place with vibrating wings and outspread and upraised tail, its lovely falcon eyes scanning the ground below for prey. If that prey be sighted there is a sudden dive, a brief pause on the ground, and then the hunter is aloft once more, after what may to human eyes appear to have been an unsuccessful stoop. But the kestrel may have been hunting beetles, and a beetle is so small a prey that it cannot be seen whether the bird has captured its quarry or not.

The love flight of a pair of kestrels above the cliff where they nest is so masterly that the birds seem to have risen beyond the earth's attraction—to be creatures on which the earth's gravity is powerless. This, most harmless of British falcons, should be protected wherever it nests, for the good to mankind it does by preying on mice, rats and voles is incalculable: yet it is too often seen nailed to a board in the gamekeeper's "larder" along with other harmless birds such as the owl, and harmful birds such as the hooded and carrion crows, the sparrow hawk and the gulls.

The *buzzard*, a heavy, rather slothful bird, is more akin to the eagles than to the falcons. Indeed, when soaring at a distance eagle and buzzard are sometimes distinguished with difficulty, although the buzzard's smaller size is at once apparent when the two species are together. I once watched a buzzard mobbing a golden eagle, and the entire buzzard was no larger than one wing of the eagle. The buzzard is not as a rule a courageous bird, and although it will not hesitate to attack the eagle when that bird flies near its nest, I have seen it having a very bad time at the hands (or should I say feet?) of a merlin. It was a female merlin which was attacking, and time after time she swooped at the unhappy buzzard, sending its feathers flying and causing it to shriek with fear.

The main food of the buzzard is the rabbit, and young rabbits are taken in preference to old. When hunting, the buzzard sometimes hovers kestrel-like, and this habit at once distinguishes it from the golden eagle, even at a distance, for the eagle, so far as my experience goes, never hovers. The buzzard seems to take all its prey on the ground, and it is interesting to record that on two occasions I have seen a stoat brought as prey to the nest. Presumably this small animal, very well able to take care of itself, was on both occasions caught unawares when dozing or asleep. Rats and mice are also taken as food for the young. Buzzards often call; eagles rarely. The buzzard's usual cry is a plaintive mewing note, and when the birds are sailing in play above a cliff or steep hillside this note is often heard.

The rough-legged buzzard, which may be distinguished from the common buzzard by its white tail, tipped with black, is a rare and irregular winter visitor from the Continent to this country.

The *hen harrier* is a large and graceful hawk with long wings and noiseless, buoyant flight which sometimes calls to mind an owl's flight. In his pure ashy-grey plumage the male is a most handsome bird, and when hunting above a moor of Orkney or the Outer Hebrides (these islands are the last strongholds of the hen harrier) he is indeed a beautiful sight. The female bird differs widely from her mate in the colour of her plumage, which is mainly dark brown. Both male and female have a pure white rump, less noticeable in the male because of the lightness of his plumage.

The hen harrier is decreasing in the Outer Hebrides, and this decrease has synchronised with the appearance on those islands of the buzzard, which was formerly unknown here. Buzzard and harrier are rarely found on the same ground, and it is quite possible that the arrival of the buzzard, and the unwelcome activities of the egg collector, are both responsible for the decrease of this fine harrier in the Outer Hebrides. In Orkney, its main stronghold at the present day, the buzzard does not nest, and the eggs of the harriers are protected as carefully as possible. I was told the following story by an Orkney bird lover, who does his best to protect the harriers' eggs, and who knows the main island so well that he is probably familiar with every nest. Hearing that a notorious egg collector had arrived at the island he visited next morning one of the harriers' nests, and arrived at the spot as the collector was putting the eggs in his pocket. A request that the eggs should be returned to the nest produced a refusal and a sarcastic remark which so roused the local protectionist's ire that his fist landed between the collector's eyes. The thief was then warned in no uncertain language that unless he left the island by the next day's boat he would have to take the consequences, and that he (the watcher) intended to be down at the pier to see that he went. The next morning a passenger with two discoloured eyes might have been seen to board the mail steamer, while a strong, determined man watched him carefully to see that he did not think better of his plan of departure.

Hen harriers lay in May. The nest is usually placed in long heather, and a nest which I saw in the summer of 1937 was in heather and rushes. This was a late nest, and at the time I was shown it (the third week in July) the young birds, although almost fully grown, were still in the nest. The mother bird was very bold in the defence of her young. She stood in the heather on the hillside about 150 yards away, and from here made a number of determined attacks on us, flying, chattering, at us with her legs stretched earthward and her claws open. My companion treated her attacks with respect and ducked his head when the bird reached him and flew past a foot or two above him, and he told me that he believed that the hen harrier was the only bird he knew which really meant business when it attacked in defence of its young. The attacks of the great skua were, he said, nearly always bluff, but since the day when a hen harrier struck his scalp with her claws, inflicting a nasty wound, he had realised that she must be treated with great respect.

The *raven* is sometimes found frequenting the same country as the hen harrier, but I do not recall having seen a sparring match between the two, although the raven is fearless and eager to attack any bird, from the golden eagle downwards, passing near its nest. There is, indeed, a pair of golden eagles nesting in

Skye whose lives must be made miserable by the continued attacks of the ravens in the district. Scarcely has one of these eagles risen above the top of the nesting cliff when, from its nest a full mile away, a raven may be seen to hurry towards the eagle, flying with repeated angry croakings at its topmost speed. The eagle, sailing leisurely upward in spirals on motionless wings, has by now reached a considerable height, and the raven may have to rise a little to the attack, but does not hesitate and rushes at the large bird with redoubled croakings. When it has reached a little height above the eagle the raven makes a slanting dive at the tip of one of the eagle's wings, but it is careful not to approach the formidable talons too closely. It is rarely that the eagle shows any impatience when suffering these unprovoked attacks, but when the great bird seems about to retaliate, the croaking of the raven, before deep and angry, now rises to a crescendo of alarm as it flees for a few seconds before the eagle. But the eagle, so far as my experience goes, never presses home the attack and the raven, as if ashamed of its cowardice, now returns to the assault with redoubled vigour. It may be that the golden eagle, a much larger and heavier bird than the raven, realises its inability to turn and twist so rapidly as the raven in mid-air and saves itself an exhausting and probably unavailing pursuit by ignoring its adversary's attacks and shouted defiance.

The raven figures largely in history and mythology. In Bosworth Smith's masterly work, *Bird Life and Bird Lore*, is to be found much raven learning. An account is given of the subterfuge of the wily commander of the army besieging Phalanthus in a town of Rhodes. Phalanthus had received tidings by an oracle that he would be able to hold the town "until ravens became white," and thus was full of confidence in his power of resisting the enemy. The commander of the besieging force had news brought him by his secret service of this cryptic utterance, and, capturing a number of ravens, rubbed their plumage with gypsum and let them loose. They flew over the town and Phalanthus, seeing them, abandoned the place in despair.

In Scandinavia the raven was the sacred bird of Odin, the god of war—he who in our language is commemorated in Wednesday or Odin's Day. The raven was held in special veneration by the Vikings, for it was Odin's own messenger and familiar friend. The war banner of the Norsemen was

54 Snipe Feeding

55 Male and Female Ring Ousels at the Nest

56 A Lesser Tern alighting beside her Eggs

fashioned in the form of a large raven. When, in a wind, the banner stiffened it then appeared as if the raven were fluttering its wings, and this was considered a happy omen. But if on the day of battle the air was still and the banner hung listlessly so that the wings appeared to droop, the omen was a serious one, for it presaged defeat.

Odin was sometimes called, as a term of great respect, "Hrafna Gwd," the Raven's God. The god had, as his special confidants, two ravens named Hugen and Munen, Mind and Memory. These ravens each morning, very early, flew abroad to gather information for the god throughout the world, and each evening returned and, perched upon his shoulders, whispered to him the information they had collected on their travels.

The Norse rovers took with them ravens when setting out on their voyages of discovery, for the raven had an uncanny sense of land even when that land was far beneath the horizon. It is narrated that Flokki, a sea-rover of renown, when he sailed out towards the north-west, to test the reports that a large unknown island lay far beyond the Faeroes, took with him three ravens, which were first solemnly consecrated to the gods.

> "He reached the Faeroes, and striking boldly out to sea beyond, let loose the first raven which, after rising high in the air, returned to the Faeroes, and thus Flokki concluded that these isles were still the nearest land. He sailed onward, and then let slip the second raven, which, after circling round for a time, returned to the war galley. Flokki then concluded that there was now no land within even a raven's sight or scent. He sailed onward once more, and then let loose the third raven, his forlorn hope. It flew off at once north-westward. Flokki followed in its wake, and discovered the eastern coast of a huge inhospitable island, which he named Iceland."

The raven is one of the first birds to nest and the eggs are laid before February is out. The nest is built on a cliff, sometimes on the coast, sometimes inland, and the nesting ledge chosen has almost always the shelter of an overhanging rock. This shelter is valuable to the brooding raven, for blizzards of snow or blinding sleet may drive along her cliff at this harsh season of the year and an eave over one's head is a comfortable thing to have. During their courtship, and indeed at every season of the year, ravens love to soar along the face of a cliff, leaning on the uprising air current. As they soar they sometimes turn with a quick movement on their backs, and fly for several seconds upside-down, righting themselves again with a second movement as quick as the first. After the young birds have left the nest the family sometimes fly up to the high hills where on occasion they soar as skilfully as eagles. Before the end of summer the parent ravens drive their brood away, and then return to their own territory which they defend against any rival pair with great tenacity. One autumn afternoon I happened to be walking near a sea cliff where each year a pair of ravens nest, and for a time stood and watched the birds sailing with masterly flight so near to one another that their wing-tips almost touched. The ravens then separated, and to my surprise both dropped almost vertically to the ground about fifty yards apart. I then noticed that a second pair of ravens were on the ground, and that each of the birds which had dropped to earth was engaged in a fierce struggle with one of the ravens on the ground. One pair of combatants rolled over and over down the steep hillside, struggling across rocks and grass with wildly flapping wings. When they came to rest the talons of one of the birds was so firmly fixed in the other that it had some difficulty in freeing itself. Both ravens then stood for a little time together, rather breathless but apparently unharmed. The pause was brief and the pursuit was continued, to the accompaniment of excited croakings, in the air, and after a time one pair of ravens flew off. I have little doubt that a strange pair had been disputing this desirable territory with the rightful owners, and had after a struggle been driven away.

It has been said by an authority on the raven that this bird has a greater fund of conscious humour than any other fowl of the air, and I believe this statement to be true, for I have more than once seen an old raven deliberately baiting a dog. The last occasion (I write in November 1937) was only a few days ago. As I was dressing, I saw from my window a collie dog rushing excitedly at top speed across a field, and noticed that the object of the dog's pursuit was a raven. The raven allowed the dog almost to reach it, then rose into the air, to fly a little way and then settle once more, looking hopefully back at the dog. The dog, annoyed and excited, again rushed to the attack. The raven again waited, then did the same thing as before. The dog, now considerably out of breath, again pursued and the game (a game at least from the raven's point of view) went on for some time.

The *grey* or *hooded crow* is a bird chiefly of Scotland although large numbers migrate from the Continent to the east coast of England in autumn and spend the winter there. This bird lacks the dignity and impressiveness of the raven. In flight it is ragged and slovenly, and in character there is little good to be said of it, unless it be that it is a wily and clever bird. It is fond of eggs, and will steal the eggs of any bird, small or large. The eggs it sometimes takes to a spring to suck, and I have seen upward of 150 eggs of sea birds sucked beside a spring on a small Hebridean island. Young birds are also taken, and a weakling lamb is not permitted to remain long alive in a district infested by hooded crows. Pennant in his *Tour in Scotland*, made in 1769, mentions that in the Hebrides on the Day of Bel-tein (May 1st, old style) it was customary to offer a propitiatory rite to creatures considered noxious. During the performance of the rite each person chanted, "This I give to thee, O Fox! Spare thou my lambs! This to thee, O Hooded Crow; this to thee, O Eagle!"

The *short-eared owl*, which is a resident and also a winter visitor to this country, is often seen abroad by day above the moors and open country where it nests. When it is left undisturbed and is not shot at this owl has little fear of man, and will sometimes attack a dog. Its slow, erratic and undulating flight is always interesting to watch, and when hunting it often drops to the ground to pick up beetles and insects besides mice and field voles. The numbers of short-eared owls may vary greatly in the same district from year to year, according to the number of mice on the ground.

This chapter on birds of the moors is growing so lengthy—the raven, I fear, is mainly responsible for this—that my remarks on the remaining six species must be brief. Of the tribe of the *snipe* I would say that they are found everywhere on the moors and lesser hills where the ground is inclined to marshiness. In Britain the great snipe is a rare visitor, and therefore the two species described will be the common snipe and the jack snipe. The common snipe nests in Britain but a large migration from the Continent takes place each autumn; the jack snipe nests in the high north, and visits us in autumn and in winter. This little snipe, sometimes called the half-snipe because of its small size, is more confiding than the common snipe and when it is disturbed flies only a few yards before settling again and at once concealing itself. The common snipe when disturbed usually flies farther, and often rises to a considerable height and disappears from view. The drumming of the snipe has furnished ornithologists with a controversial theme, but it is now generally believed that this bleating or drumming is made by the air passing through the two outermost tail feathers as the snipe plunges a few feet downwards. This theory, however, is shaken by the experience of a gamekeeper who had a tame snipe unable to fly, which, he avers, was in the habit of drumming on the ground.

It is curious that the handsome *ring ousel*, a moorland nester, should be unable to spend the winter in Britain but, like the swallow, must needs fly south, for its near relation the blackbird remains in this country throughout the year.

The ring ousel's wild song, heard in some lonely glen, is impressive, and has a melancholy quality in keeping with its surroundings. The bird has a quick, determined flight, and is bold when its nesting-haunt is disturbed, flying anxiously around the intruder and calling a loud and imperious "tack tack tack." The nest and eggs are similar to those of the blackbird, but the white gorget easily distinguishes the parent bird. In winter the ring ousel is found in the countries bordering the Mediterranean, and it is one of the first of the summer migrants to arrive in Britain, reaching the moors only a little later than the wheatear.

The *grey wagtail* usually haunts fast-flowing moorland streams. In flight its long tail, yellow breast and under tail coverts are noticeable. It is a beautiful bird, and has a quality of grace in its flight and bearing that few British birds possess. The nest is placed often near a waterfall, sometimes quite close to a dipper's nest. The grey wagtail is sometimes erroneously named the yellow wagtail, and is often confused with the true *yellow wagtail*, a summer visitor to Britain. The yellow wagtail lacks the distinctive long tail of the grey wagtail, and its back is greenish yellow as opposed to the blue-grey back of the grey wagtail.

This chapter ends with a brief account of the *twite*, a bird that is said to have been named from its call-note. The twite is a distinctive bird of the moors, and is more numerous in the west and north-west than in the east. In the Hebrides it is one of the most characteristic birds, nesting on rough pasture and moors, sometimes quite close to the sea. The eggs are small and fragile, and are spotted with red-brown on a ground colour of blue. The twite is an active little bird, and in autumn collects into flocks which fly here and there and feed on the seeds of hill grasses. A cheery little chattering song is sung, often on the wing, and this song may be heard on the most unpleasant days of summer and in winter too. Two, and sometimes even three, broods are reared, and young twites may be seen in the nest in August. The twite is not unlike a small linnet, but there is no crimson on the forehead and breast. It is sometimes called the mountain linnet. The merlin occasionally preys upon the twite, but the small bird because of its alertness frequently succeeds in escaping, and since birds have no fear of death nor knowledge of it, soon forgets the unpleasant experience.

CHAPTER V

Birds of the Lake, Loch, River and Marsh

In this chapter, which draws the net wide across the whole of Britain, I take first the *swans*, large and noble birds of snowy plumage and comparative friendliness to man.

The death song of the swan is mentioned by Chaucer, who writes of "The jealous swan, against his death that singeth," and through the years poets have written of this mysterious song. If there be indeed a swan song, it is sung not by the mute swan, which is the semi-domesticated and much the most numerous species in this country, but by the whooper swan, or the smaller Bewick's swan.

The *mute swan* can be distinguished from the whooper swan and from Bewick's swan by the colour of the bill and the carriage of the neck. The wild swans (whooper and Bewick's) hold the neck almost erect, and the bill is yellow with black markings. The mute swan holds its neck in an arch, and the colour of the bill is reddish-brown. The large black knob or "berry" at the base of the bill is characteristic of the mute swan.

Although the mute swan was originally introduced into this country it is now to all intents and purposes a truly wild bird in many districts. In the Outer Hebrides, for example, it nests on islands on many of the lochs, and on Loch Bee, in South Uist, it is no uncommon thing in summer to see a hundred and more of these birds feeding together. As this great herd of swans may be seen at the height of the nesting season the swans are presumably immature, or at all events non-nesting birds.

The mute swan is silent or almost so; the *whooper swan*, in this country mainly a winter visitor from Iceland, calls loudly and often. The whooper's call has been compared to the chiming of silver bells, and again to the sounds made by violins and trumpets. One or two pairs of whooper swans nest on highland lochs, but most of the birds arrive during October and November from Iceland, usually in small family parties. Where they are unmolested the whoopers soon become

57 A Great Crested Grebe on her Nest

58 A Mute Swan

59 A Little Grebe uncovering her Eggs

tame and are reluctant to fly from a loch on which they have taken up their winter quarters, and do not finally leave until April or even May. A few days ago I watched a small herd of these swans on a loch, and although at my approach a flock of widgeon at once took flight, the swans showed little fear.

Bewick's swan, the smallest of the three British species, nests in Siberia, and regularly visits certain lochs of the Hebrides during the winter. This swan is usually seen in larger numbers than the whooper. During a frosty spell they call repeatedly as they swim backwards and forwards without ceasing, in order to prevent ice from binding their loch. A more beautiful sight can scarcely be imagined than scores of Bewick's swans riding like small ice floes on some Hebridean loch where, as an accompaniment to their cries, is to be heard the distant roar of surf on the low, invisible shore. Yet, although there is usually no great distance between their loch and the ocean, they rarely alight on the sea, perhaps because their plumage is not adapted for salt water. Wild swans fly at deceptive speed. They almost always appear to be moving leisurely, yet their flight is powerful, and because of their size and weight they are little affected by an adverse wind.

Swans do not dive; they obtain most of their food below the surface of the water by "standing on their heads." The tribe of the *grebes* are all expert divers, and are as much at home below the surface as on it. Some of the British grebes spend their whole time on fresh water; others—the Slavonian grebe, for example, and the great crested grebe—are in winter often seen swimming at sea. Of the British grebes the largest is the great crested grebe and the smallest the little grebe, usually known as the dabchick. The *great crested grebe*, although a large bird, is of slender build, and in its nesting plumage is distinguished by its black ear tufts and white neck. In flight it appears almost white, and flies low and steadily. The nest is a floating structure, and when the sitting bird leaves her eggs, either in alarm or in order to feed, she carefully covers them over with decayed vegetable matter in order to conserve their heat during her absence.

The *Slavonian grebe* and the *black-necked grebe* are local and rare birds in most parts of the British Isles. The Slavonian grebe, a lovely bird with black forehead, crown and neck, black mantle and back, chestnut-red throat and breast, and yellow "ears" rising like small horns from beside the eyes, is found as a nesting species only on certain lochs of the Scottish highlands. Unfortunately for this bird the only loch on which it is at all numerous is the haunt of trout fishermen, and I understand that recently, because of the suspicion that the grebes feed upon infant trout, orders were given for a number to be shot. So far as I know, there was no definite proof that the grebes were feeding on the fry of trout. They do on occasion take small fish, and I myself have seen them do this, but their prey to me appeared to be small sticklebacks and minnows. But fishermen are a selfish race. They are never satisfied, even when the fishing is good: when it is bad (as it often is) they cast about in their minds to find some scapegoat. In Scotland this scapegoat may be the Slavonian grebe, or the handsome black-throated diver, or even the red-throated diver, which does its fishing in the sea and is certainly guiltless of devouring the trout of a loch. But the fishermen, after a day or two when sport is bad, say to one another, "There are too many of those confounded Slavonian grebes (or divers, or herons, or it may be some other supposed noxious species) on the loch. Something must be done about it. We must tell the keeper to thin the ranks of these vermin." Their orders are given, and the lives of beautiful and often innocent birds are ended in the hopes that more trout may be caught. Yet there are birds, such as the cormorant and certain of the gull tribe, which on occasion can undoubtedly be destructive to fresh-water fish, and if these alone were shot, no harm would result.

My wife had an unpleasant experience when photographing a Slavonian grebe at the nest. The nest was in green reeds beside a small grassy island a little way off shore. On this islet the hiding-tent was set up, and having seen my wife into the hide, with camera in position, I waded ashore through the shallow, sun-warmed water and walked along the bank of the loch, being soon out of sight of the hide. A couple of hours later I returned, and when I came in sight of the hiding-tent I saw that a herd of cattle had fed down to the shore of the loch near it. My anxiety was increased when, on a nearer approach, I saw that a bull of formidable appearance had noticed the hide, and was disapproving of it in no uncertain manner. He was standing on the shore with head down, pawing the ground. The water between the shore and the island was only a foot deep, and it looked as if any moment the bull might walk through the shallows and lift the tent and its unseen occupant, blissfully unconscious of danger, on his strong polled head. I hurried forward at my best speed, and took a short cut across to the island, forestalling the bull who now had become furious and was kept at bay with difficulty by our collie, Dileas. The dismantling of hide and camera was done on this occasion, as may be imagined, more speedily than usual, and the farmer arriving providentially on the scene averted what had threatened to develop into a crisis.

Young grebes swim confidently from the day of their birth, and may sometimes be seen having a ride on their mother's or father's back. When the parent dives the young grebes fall off her, and swim forlornly alone on the water, often far from land. It seems likely that they are sometimes eaten by large pike on these occasions, but their parent is soon on the surface once more after the dive, and carries usually in her bill a small fish, or water-beetle, or aquatic larva, which she has caught for the children.

Of the black-necked grebe I have no personal knowledge. In Ireland it suddenly arrived in considerable numbers on a small lough some years ago, but the lake dried and the grebes disappeared.

The *little grebe* is the smallest, and most numerous, of British grebes, and is found on suitable sheets of water throughout the British Isles. It is a friendly little bird, adept, as all grebes are, at swimming and diving. It is a partial migrant, and in winter may go from its fresh-water haunts of summer down to the sea or to some river estuary where it remains until spring.

The true *divers* swim low, dive without a splash—this latter characteristic distinguishes them from cormorant and shag—and are able to swim far and fast below the surface. Their flight is straight and swift, and the neck when the bird is flying is held in a slight downward curve that is very characteristic. Three species of divers are found in British waters—the great northern diver, the black-throated diver and the red-throated diver. The largest of the three, the *great northern diver*, is as large as a goose. This diver is a winter visitor to Britain, and there is no proof that it has ever nested with us. Great northern divers may indeed be seen in full breeding plumage at midsummer at sea off the Scottish coast, and I have more than once received information that a pair of great northern divers have been found nesting on some highland loch, but upon investigation the so-called great northern diver has been found to be the black-throated diver.

There is a curious belief, strongly held by most fishermen, that the great northern diver is incapable of flight. This belief may have grown because of the fact that this diver is almost always seen swimming and diving, yet on occasion it *can* fly fast and far. One winter day the mail boat from Skye to the mainland almost ran down a great northern diver, which came to the surface only a few feet from the swiftly moving bows of the vessel. The diver had no time to dive, and without a second's pause took wing, and after flying a little way made a diagonal gannet-like plunge—a crash dive which I have never before seen the species make. The great northern diver nests in Iceland and in Greenland, and also in Canada. The birds which winter in British waters are in no hurry to leave for their northern haunts and may be seen frequenting the strong tide races above a sandy bottom until mid-May. Perhaps because the egg was never seen, there was a curious old belief that this diver not only laid its egg but hatched it beneath the water's surface, in the country of the fish on which it preys. The usual Gaelic name for the great northern diver is *bun a' bhuachaille*, the herdsman of the tide-race, and indeed the bird is at home on the swiftest ocean current. This diver dives to a great depth for its fish, and I have frequently timed one to remain below the surface for a minute and a half. Below the surface the great northern diver travels at incredible speed, but on the surface it never swims fast and dives instantly when alarmed. The white throat-band and "collar" of the great northern diver in the nesting plumage distinguish that bird (apart altogether from its larger size) from the black-throated diver, with which it is sometimes confused.

The *black-throated diver* is one of the most handsome of British-nesting birds. In Britain it nests only on the fresh-water lochs of the Scottish highlands, and were it not for the activities of egg collectors and fish preservers would undoubtedly increase. Black-throated divers arrive in spring at their nesting loch. The arrival has not, so far as I am aware, been seen—it probably takes place at night—but one morning the divers are noticed swimming with stately measure on their loch. When the loch is high among the hills frost may sometimes bind the water after the arrival of the divers. I remember one morning early in April looking out from my bedroom window at the margin of a hill loch and seeing the waters frozen firmly with a sheet of black ice and the black-throated divers, swimming leisurely,

60 A Ringed Plover with her Eggs

61 A Male Red-necked Phalarope settling on the Eggs

62 Oyster Catchers at the Nest

63 A Sandpiper and her Chick

keeping open a swimming-pool. I have not heard of these birds being frozen in after their arrival, for April frosts are usually transient. Divers are able to progress with great difficulty on land, and therefore lay their eggs as close to the water as is possible. They endeavour to find a site on the bank of a loch from which, springing from the eggs on the approach of danger, they are able to dive noiselessly into the water. I have never seen a diver *fly* from the nest. The black-throated diver nests usually on a small island on a loch, and lays two large dark eggs. When, after heavy rains, the loch rises, these eggs may be washed into the water and lost, but more often during the nesting period the loch shrinks, and the diver as she broods finds herself being left farther and farther from the friendly water. The legs of the diver are set far back, and cannot support the weight of the body, and the bird as it attempts to walk falls forward, and progresses painfully on its breast. It must be remembered that the tribe of the true divers never come to land except during the weeks that the eggs are being incubated. The day they are hatched the young take to the water and remain there until they are able to fly, and from that time the water and the air are their home until in their turn they come ashore to nest.

The *red-throated diver* is a smaller bird than the black-throated diver, and is found nesting usually on the shore of a small tarn. It is never numerous as a British-nesting species, and its main strongholds are the north-west coast of Scotland and the Hebrides. In winter this species, like the great northern diver and the black-throated diver, makes its home on the sea, sometimes as far south as the Mediterranean.

On a summer's evening when flying from its tarn to the sea to fish the red-throated diver utters a rapidly repeated loud quacking. This bird seems to embody the spirit of the lonely isles and hill-set coastline. Its swift, undeviating flight when seen against the afterglow of the Hebridean sky in June at midnight is a mysterious thing, and its cry, wild and compelling, might come from one of the *uruisgean* or *gruagachan* which in tradition and folk-lore people those seagirt isles.

The *phalaropes*, attractive and confiding birds in size a little smaller than the dunlin, and differing from it and from other waders in having lobed feet, nest only in wild, unfrequented places usually near but never on, the sea. Of the two species which may be seen in Britain the *grey*, or as it might more appropriately be termed the *black-capped phalarope*, nests in the Arctic regions and is a passage migrant to this country. The *red-necked phalarope* is a summer visitor and makes its summer home in the west of Ireland, in one of the Inner and several of the Outer Hebrides, in Orkney and in Shetland. The red-necked phalarope deserves special mention if only for its remarkable courtship. In most birds the male is the courtier: in the red-necked phalarope he is the courted. The lady phalarope, as befits her role, is larger and more beautifully plumaged than the male. She is a vehement lover, and will on occasion pursue the smaller and reluctant male this way and that, in the water and in the air, until he submits to her attentions. After she has laid her four richly marked eggs the female phalarope takes no further interest in them, and for nineteen days (this was the incubation period of a nest which my wife and I had under observation) the cock bird broods his wife's eggs. During all that time she does not, so far as is known, come near him, nor take any interest in the fate of her eggs. Her harassed husband has no light task, for common gulls are often on the look-out for unguarded eggs, which they consider a great delicacy, and the phalarope, as he broods in the grass beside the loch, draws with his bill dried grasses over his back as a shield against aerial enemies. Before the eggs are laid, cock and hen phalaropes swim buoyantly together on their reedy loch, making sudden swift rushes after some insect their quick eyes have spied on the water's surface. Sometimes they rise from the water and flit, with rapid, swallow-like flight, backwards and forwards, but they are rarely in the air for long and soon alight on the loch with a perfection of grace that is scarcely seen in any other water bird.

Egg collectors are sometimes blamed for the rarity of the red-necked phalarope, but I am inclined to believe that, in the Hebrides at all events, cattle do more harm to the nests of these birds than collectors. In the Hebrides the crofters' cattle are usually under the charge of a herdsman who is paid by the township, and the animals graze in large flocks. On warm summer days, when the phalaropes are nesting, the cattle in scores—perhaps in hundreds—go to the loch to drink. They then graze on the succulent grasses where the phalaropes are brooding, and even if they do not tramp on the eggs they remove by their eager grazing the shelter these small birds have against their enemies the gulls. If areas here and there beside the nesting lochs of the phalaropes were to be fenced in against cattle I have little doubt that the birds would increase.

In August the phalaropes fly south. The sea is their thoroughfare, and over the Atlantic waves they swiftly fly, wintering, often far out of sight of land, in the region of the Azores or even south of that latitude.

The *dunlin* must be familiar to many people who are not particularly interested in birds because of its habit of frequenting, often in large flocks, sandy shores throughout the British Isles. The dunlin is a small wader that is possessed of an endless store of restless energy. During its feeding hours it is scarcely still for a moment. Each receding wave is actively followed up for the food it has left, and at each oncoming wave the birds are driven back, running at their topmost speed, but rarely flying unless the sea is stormy and the speed of the waves unusually fast. During the height of the tide, when their feeding-grounds are submerged, the dunlins sometimes fly out to a little spit of land, or to a low island, and standing so close together that they almost, or quite, touch, doze away the short hour or two until the tide is at the ebb. There is no bird which gives me quite the same impression of restless energy when feeding except, perhaps, the starling. The dunlins which we in Britain see on the shore in winter are chiefly immigrants from countries to the north-east: our British-nesting dunlins in winter are probably feeding on the shores of Portugal or Spain, or Africa. As a nesting species the dunlins of Britain have two distinct habits: some of them nest near the sea and almost at sea level, but others make their summer home on the high hills, where, on the Cairngorms, I have frequently seen them nesting 3,000 feet and more above the level of the sea. The nest is placed usually in a tussock of grass, and four pear-shaped eggs are laid. The dunlin rarely flies from the nest but runs furtively, when you are still some distance away, through the grass, so that you rarely see her go. The nest is therefore difficult to find, and the more often you visit the place and disturb her, the more furtively will she slip from the eggs and be gone literally without a trace. When the eggs are hatched, the dunlin becomes a most anxious mother, and runs round you, uttering a curious throaty call, "Oick oick oick oick," but rarely rising into the air. In the Hebrides dunlins, like phalaropes, are almost continuously harried by common gulls, and I have seen a common gull alight at a dunlin's nest and swallow the four eggs one after another, so quickly that the last of them was gone before I could rise to my feet and drive the villain away. The common gull, a small gull of innocent, dove-like appearance, is not the only culprit, for I once saw a black-headed gull swallow a newly hatched dunlin chick before my eyes. I was photographing a dunlin on her nest from a hiding tent, and was watching her through a small peephole in the front of the hide when I saw her suddenly crouch on the nest and then with a terrified demeanour creep off it. My view was restricted, and before I realised what was happening a black-headed gull had swooped down on the nest, lifted a small dunlin in its beak, and swallowed it instantly. Not long afterwards the gull was back again, for a second tit-bit. The dunlin as before first crouched on the nest, then crept off it, and the gull was just about to alight and swallow the second infant dunlin when I shouted my loudest and waved my hand through the peephole. The black-headed gull, badly scared, sheered off, and I thought that I had seen the last of it, but the recollection of that tender food was too much for it, and it soon returned, flying backwards and forwards above the nest, and causing the brooding dunlin much anxiety. I feared that the hiding-tent was a landmark for the marauder, and so after a time I took down the hide and left the place, covering over the nest as far as possible with the dead grass where it was situated before I walked away.

In summer plumage the dunlin is distinguished by its black breast which is lost after the nesting season, like the black breast of the golden plover. Its food in winter is mainly small shrimps and sandhoppers and, in summer, worms, snails and insects.

Among the dunlins which on a winter day haunt the low wet shore beneath a grey, storm-swept sky a number of slightly larger, and less eager and impetuous birds are sometimes seen. These are *ringed plovers*, called by old Willughby "sealarks." These small waders, of robust form and more upright carriage than the dunlin, are characteristic birds, not only of the British coasts but of certain highland rivers and inland lochs. It is probable that the British-nesting ringed plovers move south at the approach of winter, for the species flies south in winter as far as Cape Colony.

The bold black and white markings of the ringed plover are distinctive: in winter, on the shore, it might possibly be mistaken by the novice for a turnstone, but its legs are yellow, and the legs of the turnstone are pink.

In summer the male ringed plover has, like its larger relative the golden plover, a characteristic song-flight. This flight takes place at a lower altitude than the golden plover's flight, but like the golden plover, the ringed plover slows down his usual quick wing-thrusts; his strokes become slow and wavering, and his flight erratic and not unlike that of the stormy petrel. Backwards and forwards over the nesting ground he swerves and wheels, then suddenly sinks to earth, closes his wings and becomes at once invisible.

The ringed plover's nest, if nest it can be called, is a shallow depression scraped in short-cropped grass, sand or shingle. The eggs resemble their surroundings in a remarkable manner, and might easily be trodden under foot.

A summer haunt of the ringed plover which I know well is a pine-encircled loch lying at the base of the Cairngorm Hills. At the east end of this loch is a shore of golden sand and gravel, and each spring a pair of ringed plovers arrive to nest. As the male circles in graceful courtship flight above the clear, amber-coloured waters of the loch, he sees—has he an eye for such things—the snowy slopes of the Cairngorms rise to the May sky and is perhaps for a moment alarmed by the dull roar of the avalanche which each year towards the end of May sweeps down the smooth rocks of Coire an Lochain. The ringed plovers here have oyster catchers for their companions, and hear sometimes the cry of the greater spotted woodpecker coming from old pines, and of an evening see the clan of the goosander hunt the trout of the loch, and at earliest dawn, when the air, even at midsummer, is chill, hear the bubbling, challenging notes of blackcock, rising and falling in cadences. When at noon the sun shines high in the heavens and beats down upon the unshaded sand until it is hot to the touch, the ringed plover pants on the four precious eggs which must be shielded equally from heat and cold, and sees the green plovers which nest in the grass lands to the east fly across the heated, scented pines and settle beside the loch to drink and to cool themselves. She hears the cheery song of the chaffinches in the pines, and the sorrowful music of willow warblers in the birches where drooping boughs sway in the fitful breeze and leaves are turned to silver as they lean to the sun.

But these ringed plovers are unusual in their surroundings.

More often than not the nesting site is beside the sea, and, on two occasions the tide of a sea loch of the Isle of Mull rose so high that the eggs were washed from a ringed plover's nest on the shore of the loch. I visited the nesting site shortly after high tide—too late, unfortunately, to save the eggs—and saw the ringed plover flying anxiously over her empty nest, apparently unable to believe that her eggs were gone. The pair soon nested again, and the hen bird laid four more eggs. The new nest was on shingle, beside the ruins of an old boathouse. It was unfortunate that the neap tides were on when the hen bird laid, for during the neaps the tide does not rise high. When I found the nest I saw that the eggs were in a dangerous place, and when the "springs" approached my wife and I kept the nest under observation during the evening high tides—which in the Hebrides are almost always higher than the morning tides. Each day the tides rose higher, and each day the sea water crept a little nearer to the home of *tarmachan na tuinne*, the ptarmigan of the waves, as the ringed plover is poetically named in Gaelic. One afternoon the top of the tide was only a few inches from the eggs, and we were convinced that next day the eggs would float out to sea. My wife, therefore, reached the shore next afternoon before high water. She watched the sea water rise to the nest, and when it began to trickle into it she lifted the eggs and carried them up the shore, replacing them an hour later when the tide receded. Next morning at six o'clock (the highest tides both morning and evening are around six o'clock) I visited the nest, but the morning's tide did not reach it. We were obliged to be from home that day, and it was high water when we returned. I hurried to the shore—too late. The nest was flooded, and the eggs had been drifted out into the loch by the strong wind blowing off the land. Thus twice in a few short weeks that pair of ringed plovers lost their eggs.

Oyster catcher and ringed plover usually nest on the same kind of ground. A beautiful, attractive bird, the oyster catcher is burdened with an absurd name. Whoever heard of any bird *catching* oysters! These sedentary bivalves are not hard to catch: oyster picker, would indeed be a better name, and it is indeed one of the local names of this bird. But the oyster catcher does *not* feed on oysters. Its name in earlier works (Kay, 1570, and Willughby, 1678) is sea pie. The name oyster catcher was first used for the American species, and was

64 A Dipper, photographed by flashlight

65 A Moorhen at the Nest

66 A Redshank at the Nest

67 A Male Reed Bunting at the Nest

68 A Sand Martin at the Nesting Hole

69 A Bittern at the Nest

70 Young Bitterns

introduced to this country by Pennant. The Gaelic name for the oyster catcher is *gille Bride*, Bride's servant. Saint Bride took the bird under her special protection because of an act of kindness which it performed long, long ago. Christ, in this old Celtic legend, was in flight from His inexorable enemies, and during this flight through the Isles reached a shore that was bare and shelterless. It seemed as if His capture was certain, but one oyster catcher said to the other, "That shall not be," and together the pair covered Christ over with sea-weed, so that His enemies passed Him by. It was little wonder that Bride, patron saint of beauty and of fire, adopted the oyster catcher, which became her personal servant. The oyster catcher can be distinguished by its bold black and white plumage and its long and straight orange-red bill. Like the ringed plover, it nests sometimes on the coast, sometimes far up highland rivers and on the shores of lochs. Although it nests in England—I have seen eggs on the Farne Islands in August—it is more numerous in Scotland, where in spring and summer it is found along most of the great rivers—Spey and Dee, Tay and many others. In winter, oyster catchers move south as far as Africa, and it is probable that our river-nesting birds when they arrive late in February have flown far from the south. They are seen first on the lower reaches of the rivers, and they evidently enter the river from the coast, which they have followed on their northward flight. Spring has scarcely arrived when they appear, and they are in no hurry to fly up-stream to their inland nesting haunts, which at that season may be deep in snow. On the Spey and the Dee a month and more may elapse between the time of the oyster catchers entering the river valley and the arrival of the birds at their spring haunts at the upper reaches of the main river and along its highland tributaries, where some of the oyster catchers nest at a height of 1,500 feet above the sea.

During the spring and early summer months oyster catchers play an amusing game. With heads bent so that the tips of the bills almost touch the ground the birds, to the number of half a dozen and more, run quickly over the short grass or shingle, all the time uttering excited short, high-pitched whistling cries which after a time almost die away, and then break out afresh with greater clamour than ever. This game, for such it undoubtedly is, is entered into with zest by any oyster catcher that happens to be in the neighbourhood. Like the golden plover and other waders the oyster catcher has a love song that is uttered on the wing. In his normal flight, the oyster catcher moves his wings very fast, but as he begins his aerial song, "ko-beeak, ko-beeak," the character of the flight is at once altered, and the wings are moved slowly, in rhythm with his two-syllabled cry.

Oyster catchers usually lay three eggs: they make no nests, but a hollow is scraped in the grass, heather, shingle, or sand, and is lined sometimes with pebbles, sometimes with shells, sometimes with dried rabbit droppings—these are a favourite lining—and sometimes with buds or flowers of the sea thrift.

The *sandpiper*, sometimes called the summer snipe, is often seen nesting on the same ground as the oyster catcher. This cheery little bird arrives considerably later at its summer haunts than the oyster catcher, and is most regular in the date of its arrival from its African winter quarters. It can be looked for about April 20th on the rivers and streams with which I am familiar, and its high-pitched song, "titty teetie, titty teetie," uttered as the singer flies on quivering wings driven at a very fast speed, brings a new joy to many a river and stream. It is delightful, also, to see the first sandpiper tripping daintily along the river bank, curtseying with airy grace and showing great happiness at being back at home once more after that long northward flight of thousands of miles, over land and sea. To watch sandpipers courting on a summer evening above their nesting haunts on lake, loch, stream or river is to see the most delicately graceful flying I know; the ethereal quality of the song is also unusual.

The *redshank*, an excitable bird, for which an old name was the red-legged horseman, is more partial to bogs and swamps than to running water. It is a bird of the coast in winter, and in summer nests indifferently on coastal and inland marshes. The usual flight of the redshank is erratic and swift: the wing-thrusts are very powerful, especially when the bird first rises from the ground. The courtship flight of the redshank during the singing of the spring song is almost lark-like, the singer rising into the breeze and after remaining poised for a few seconds, descending rapidly to earth, all the time making loud music. During the upward flight the song is a clear whistling "clu, clu, clu," and changes to "clueu, clueu, clueu" during the downward soaring. The alarm note is sharp and short, and the redshank also uses a call note sounding like "teuk a took too". The redshank lays four beautiful pear-shaped eggs, richly marked with reddish brown spots. Unlike the oyster catcher, which lays in the open, the redshank conceals her nest carefully in a tussock of grass. During the winter months when redshanks haunt our coasts they do not, like most waders, feed altogether below high-water mark, but often fly in from the shore to the fields and grass lands near the sea. In the Hebrides these birds are mainly, if not entirely, winter visitors, probably from Scandinavia.

It is curious that the *dipper* or water ousel should in Gaelic be named *an gobha dubh*, the blacksmith. This cheery little bird, dapper and white-breasted, often stands on a boulder of some brawling stream or more quietly flowing river, and as he stands there, perhaps in midstream, repeatedly bows or curtseys, or dips, hence the bird's name, dipper. Dippers are allied to wrens, and the song, which is sung at the heart of winter as well as in early spring, bears a slight resemblance to a wren's song, but is more musical and dreamy.

No one who is familiar with this dapper little bird, of rotund form, can fail to be impressed by its complete confidence in the water. Not only can it dive in a raging torrent, but it is able to walk actually on the bed of a river, where, several feet beneath the surface, it turns over small stones and picks up the water larvae which are its chief food. The human observer never quite loses the thrill of seeing a dipper fly in through a waterfall to its nest. It makes light of this passage through what looks like an almost solid wall of water, and, having fed the family in their domed nest darts out through the fall and flies away, without even a shake of the feathers, up, or down, the stream in search of more food. But skilled in aquatic arts though the dipper is, it is powerless to protect its nest when a flood roars down the burn, and often the nest with its white glossy eggs or its callow young is washed away in the torrent.

There are fishermen who would destroy the dipper because they believe that on occasion it feeds on the ova of trout and salmon. The bird, it is true, often haunts spawning beds in a stream, but I have seen it also on shallow gravelly stretches of water so high above the sea level that no fish frequent them—as, for example, beside the Wells of Dee on the Cairngorm Hills where the dipper in early autumn may sometimes be seen 4,000 feet above the sea, feeding, certainly not on the spawn of fish, for no fish are here, but probably on aquatic larvae or beetles, which are most harmful to fish spawn. The dipper is one of the earliest birds to nest, and I have seen the nest ready for eggs on February 11th.

Moorhen and *coot* haunt lakes and slow-flowing rivers. At first sight the word moorhen seems most inappropriate for a bird which rarely indeed is seen on a moor, but the word *moor* is believed to be derived, in this instance, from the Anglo-Saxon word *mor*, meaning a bog or morass, and thus the bird's name is in reality not unsuitable. The red frontal shield and bright red bill of the moorhen are handsome and striking when the bird is seen at close quarters. At Fallodon the late Viscount Grey used to tame the moorhens of the place: they had little fear of man and used to take bread from his hand. He told me that one season a pair of moorhens reared two broods, and towards the end of that nesting season the parent moorhen used to take food from his hand, pass the food to her full-grown brood, and these in turn with exemplary unselfishness would pass the food on to their smaller brothers and sisters. Most young birds, once they have left the shelter of the parental home, do not return to it, but moorhens are devoted and united families, and the young each night return to roost in the nest for some time after they are fully grown. When the moorhen is seen at close quarters the feet seem too large for the bird, and give it the appearance of wearing boots.

The coot is a larger bird than the moorhen, and frequents more open water. Against its black plumage the white shield on its forehead is conspicuous, and it swims and dives actively, often in large flocks. This bird finds it none too easy to take wing from the water, and its legs for some little distance are used as aids to its wings, and give their owner the appearance of racing on the water with great strides. The coots which throng the Norfolk Broads in thousands in winter are mostly immigrants from the Continent.

The *bittern*, formerly a nesting species in many parts of the British Isles, was at one time esteemed a delicacy for the table, and in Montagu's day (1802) was valued by poulterers at half-a-guinea. The bittern soon decreased in numbers and the last nest recorded in its Norfolk stronghold was in 1868, although in 1886 a young bird with down upon it was found there. In 1911 bird lovers were excited at the report of Miss E. L. Turner that the bittern was once more nesting in Norfolk and at the present day the bird, now strictly protected, breeds

71 A Pair of Reed Warblers and their Family

72 Montagu's Harrier with her Young

73 Young Kingfishers

on the Norfolk Broads in increasing numbers. The deep bellow of the male bittern carries far: its slow and owl-like flight is characteristic. The bittern is an adept at concealing itself in reed beds, in which it stands erect and motionless with bill pointing vertically skyward: it is seldom seen in flight during the day except when there are young in the nest to feed.

The *bearded tit* haunts the reed beds with the bittern. This small graceful bird rarely flies far from the reeds, but although it is a resident at its nesting haunts, a hard winter reduces its numbers greatly and in the early part of 1936 when I visited its nesting haunts in Norfolk very few bearded tits were to be seen.

The *marsh warbler* sings vociferously by night as well as by day. The song is striking and melodious. The *reed warbler's* song has been likened to a babbling chatter. In the song of the *sedge warbler* are harsh notes which serve to distinguish it. The *reed bunting*, another frequenter of reed beds and boggy land, is a pleasant, cheerful bird, and its black head and throat and white collar serve to identify it.

Of the reed-haunting harriers, which prey on these small birds, the *hen harrier* is a winter visitor to the Norfolk Broads, and the *marsh harrier* and *Montagu's harrier* are the two species usually seen in summer. Montagu's harrier is not unlike the hen harrier in appearance, but is of more slender build. It feeds mainly on small birds, but takes also frogs and snakes. The marsh harrier, the largest British harrier, is slower in flight than the other species, and its wings are more rounded. It is a beautiful bird, the head white, the wing primaries black and the rest of the plumage a rich brown. Very strict preservation has increased the numbers of this rare harrier in the Norfolk Broads, but in the last year or two (I write in 1937) the species has mysteriously decreased during the nesting season, and there is little doubt that the birds have been shot or trapped as they searched for food on neighbouring game preserves.

Sometimes a larger and more splendid bird than the marsh harrier is seen fishing on the Norfolk Broads. The *osprey*, for such it is, may remain only a few days and may be seen plunging magnificently beneath the water for the fish on which it preys. The osprey may be on passage to or from Scandinavia; in Britain, sad to relate, it is now extinct as a nesting species. Loch Arkaig, Loch an Eilein, and Loch Loyne were the three last nesting haunts of the osprey in Scotland, and the last nest in the highlands of which I have a record was in 1910, when one young bird was hatched, and, so far as was known, left the eyrie safely. But wandering ospreys still pay us occasional visits, and in recent years an osprey stayed for a fortnight on a river on the Duke of Portland's Langwell estate, and became very tame.

The *water rail's* headquarters are in Norfolk. It is a bird, secretive like the bittern, haunting the reed beds, and sometimes is seen swimming like a miniature moorhen. In Scotland it is rare as a nester, and was not known to nest north of the Grampians until a friend of mine recorded a water rail, killed by chance on Upper Strathspey, which had in its oviduct eggs ready for laying.

The *kingfisher* is unique among British birds in the brilliance of its colouring. Its dazzling cobalt-blue upper parts and reddish-brown under plumage, its short form and its bullet-like flight—all these are unmistakable. The kingfisher is a bird of rivers, but is sometimes seen on the coast during the winter months. There is a very old belief that the kingfisher made her nest of fish bones and launched it on the ocean, and that while she brooded her eggs and young on the waters the halcyon or kingfisher days of fine weather were provided by the Spirit of Ocean in order that the young kingfishers might be reared safely in their floating ocean home. How this strange belief originated it is difficult to conceive unless it be that the eggs of the kingfisher, being laid at the end of a tunnel in the vertical mud bank of a stream, were rarely if ever seen.

Like the kingfisher, the *sand martin* tunnels out its home, sometimes on the bank of a stream, sometimes on the face of a gravel pit. The sand martin is a smaller bird than the swallow or the house martin, and its brown back at once identifies it. It arrives in Britain from its African winter haunts earlier than the swallow and considerably earlier than the house martin, and is sometimes seen before March is out. Should the spring be inclement the sand martins become torpid in their burrows, and many succumb if the cold spell should be prolonged.

The *heron*, a harsh-voiced, long-legged bird which, according to Turner "routs eagles or hawks, if they attack it suddenly, by very liquid mutings of the belly," spends most of its life in marshes, or wading stealthily in lakes, lochs and rivers. It is therefore curious that this bird should nest usually in high trees. On a Hebridean island, where the herons have no enemies, the birds make their nests and lay their sky-blue unspotted eggs in the reed beds of a loch, choosing the same nesting site that a coot might do and it is possible that the heron was originally a ground-nesting bird like the crane, and that much persecution caused it to fly to the tree-tops to rear its family, for on lofty trees it always seems to be out of place. In the Hebrides, where trees are scarce, I have known a colony of herons nest on one small oak growing beside a waterfall: by standing above the waterfall it was possible to look down upon the nests with their eggs and young. Many young herons fall from the nest during the early days of their lives. The herons nest very early—sometimes in February—and the equinoctial gales frequently blow the nests to the ground, and more often agitate them so violently that the young are thrown out, and die on the earth below the trees. Although the chief food of the heron is fish, caught with much skilled stalking, the fisherman sometimes turns his attention to young birds, and the lighthouse-keepers of the Copeland Islands tell me that when the young terns are hatched, herons often fly over from the mainland of Northern Ireland and pick up and devour any unguarded nestling.

CHAPTER VI

Birds of the Sea-Coast and Islands

THERE is a magic quality in spring days. The air is vital, and although the grass beside the sea is green those conical hills away on the northern horizon rise deep in snow to the blue sky. Each morning the sun climbs a little higher toward the zenith: each morning his rays in sunny island nooks shine more warmly. Small red buds are seen on the green cushions of the sea thrift: the leaves of the sea campion become green and succulent and the flower buds swell: a mirage dances above the shingle beds at the margin of which a line of brown sea wrack floats.

It is on a day such as this that the tribe of *guillemot* and *razorbill* arrive from ocean solitudes at their island, and in scores, in hundreds, in thousands alight on their nesting cliffs, crowding so thickly that there appears to be no more room, even for a single new arrival. But still the birds come, alighting on the back of their fellows and waddling, to the accompaniment of grunts and shrieks of disapproval, over a living pathway until they squeeze into some cranny, and make the press of birds still more solid. The guillemots grunt and groan and shriek; local quarrels spring to life and gradually die away. This crowded, communal life of the guillemot during the nesting season appears, and perhaps is, uncomfortable, yet its main advantage is that the birds, nesting thus in crowded ranks, are comparatively safe from the inroads of their enemies—of which the herring gull is the chief. When given its opportunity, by the disturbance of a guillemot colony, a herring gull will fly in and gobble up a guillemot's egg or small chick in less time than it takes to tell of the crime.

The *guillemot* is an auk and, a true ocean bird, is out of its element on land, which it frequents only during the nesting season. Its legs, adapted for swimming and diving, are with difficulty able to support the bird on land, and it is hard for a guillemot to stand erect, if only for a second.

The egg of the guillemot, enormous for the size of the bird, is laid on a bare ledge of rock. No attempt at a nest is made,

74 A Stormy Petrel with her Egg

75 Guillemots on the Farne Islands

and the bird when brooding holds the egg sometimes on its feet, penguin-like. The egg is pear-shaped, and is often very beautifully marked. When the young guillemots come to be hatched, they are so numerous, and are so close together, that it must be a most difficult thing for each parent to recognise its offspring: it is indeed believed that on occasions communal feeding takes place. I have sometimes watched a guillemot arrive from sea with a fish in its bill, and noticed the extreme reluctance of the bird brooding the young to uncover its charge for the feeding. The guillemot brooding the young seems to be jealous: it is only by the exercising of much patience that the fish-bringer is in the end permitted to deliver the food, which the youngster swallows eagerly. The fish is sometimes so large that the little guillemot literally stiffens as the food passes down its throat. The young guillemot leaves the ledge for the sea before it is able to fly, and as the ledge may on occasion be as high as 500 feet above the sea that first great leap must indeed be perilous. It is believed that the parent bird long encourages the chick before it will launch itself on its small and undeveloped wings out over the abyss. Its fluttering wing stumps may have just sufficient strength to carry it clear of the jagged projecting rocks, but all the young guillemots do not reach the ocean safely, and on one occasion when my wife and I were rowed round the cliffs of Mingulay in the Outer Hebrides, where some of the guillemots nest more than 500 feet above the sea, we saw many downy birds floating lifeless on the swell beneath the rocks.

The *razorbill* is often confused with the guillemot, but at close quarters may readily be distinguished by the deep bill with its white diagonal stripes. The razorbill deserves notice, if only because of its close relationship with the great auk, a bird which bred on the St. Kilda group of islands until 1840 or thereabouts. The great auk, being flightless and being greatly esteemed as food by the St. Kildans (they hung the great auk in the peat smoke and stuffed it full of the fat of other seabirds which they killed) quickly became exterminated. Its smaller relative the razorbill, having the power of flight and being less esteemed as a delicacy, remains with us, and is found in considerable numbers (though not so plentifully as the guillemot) on most British cliffs and islands. It prefers rough, stony ground to sheer cliffs, and relies for protection more on the sheltered sites it chooses than on communal nesting like the guillemot. The razorbill is a more intelligent bird than the guillemot, whose brains are limited, and I have not known its egg or young fall a victim to a marauding gull. It is a quieter bird than the guillemot: it does not shriek harshly in anger, and its cry, infrequently uttered, is a long-drawn snore. It is a curious thing that when a young guillemot, or a young razorbill, is seen at sea it is never—so far as my experience goes—accompanied by *both* parents, but always by a single adult bird. It would seem that one of the parents leaves the chick after it moves off the rock into the ocean, and it is perhaps the mother that tends it during the subsequent weeks and months of adolescence.

Guillemots in recent years have been divided by ornithologists into two races, the northern guillemot, which is the Scottish form—this is distinguished by the deeper black of the back plumage and in the summer by the deeper chocolate of the throat and head—and the southern guillemot, which is the English form.

The *black guillemot* is less numerous than the common guillemot. It is a pigeon-like bird with a large white wing patch and bright red legs and feet. In winter the black guillemot assumes an almost white plumage. In its habits it is less a bird of the ocean than the common guillemot, and spends most of its time in bays and around the islands where it nests. This guillemot breeds in small scattered colonies: it lays two eggs, and they are placed usually beneath a boulder or down a hole. The same site is used year after year, and the eggs are laid regularly on or about the first of June. The young of the black guillemot remain in the nesting-place until they are feathered, and are fed on small gurnards and flounders, and on young congers.

When their nesting island is invaded by human beings the parent black guillemots sometimes swim backwards and forwards in line, uttering high and shrill whistling cries.

The *puffin* is one of the most distinctive and quaint of our sea birds. During the nesting season the puffin sports a bill so large and brightly coloured as to be almost grotesque. A local name for the puffin, given it because of this gaudy bill, is the sea parrot. The puffin is a bird of the Atlantic coasts of Britain rather than of the east, and on the east coast of England has only two breeding stations—the Farne Islands in Northumberland and Flamborough Head in Yorkshire. In winter the puffin is rarely seen along our coasts, and when the birds arrive off their nesting islands in April they are already paired. For a week and more after they come they keep the sea, as though reluctant to set foot on land after their nine months on the ocean. But once they have touched land they appear to find it very pleasant, and of an evening in early May the birds may be seen, like pompous butlers, standing importantly at their front doors, taking the air. The business of excavating a new burrow or repairing the old necessitates hard work and frequent pauses for breath and fresh air at the mouth. One egg is laid in May, and when the young bird is hatched it is fed frequently on the fry of fish, or on sand eels, which may be carried a considerable distance from the fishing grounds to the nesting island. A pair of greater black-backed gulls do an immense amount of harm to a puffin colony when they nest near it. This large gull is quite ruthless and merciless, and tears out the entrails of the unfortunate puffins which it captures at their nesting burrows: the victims are left to perish miserably. During the late summer of 1937 I saw near a greater black-back's nest scores of puffin remains lying on the rocks. Most of the birds had been neatly skinned and turned inside out. White, or almost white, puffins are sometimes seen.

There are no more pleasing and graceful birds than the *terns*, often called, because of their flight, sea swallows. In Britain are found nesting the sandwich tern, the common tern, the roseate tern, the Arctic tern, and the lesser tern: the black tern is an occasional spring visitor.

Terns are lovely birds; their wings are long and pointed, and the tail is deeply forked, the outer tail feathers being considerably longer than the rest. These birds are all summer visitors and do not, like the wheatear and the chiffchaff, arrive before the last sting of winter is over, but linger above tropic seas until May. The exception is the largest and strongest of British terns, the sandwich tern, which I have seen off the Farne Islands, where a considerable colony nest, at the end of March and more commonly in April.

The *sandwich tern* lacks some of the grace of the other terns, and at a distance it is not unlike a small black-headed gull: it plunges deeper into the sea after its prey than the smaller terns. The *roseate tern*, a tern with most graceful, buoyant flight and breast suffused with a pale rosy shade, is the rarest of British terns. One colony nests on a small island of the Irish Sea.

A lighthouse stands on the neighbouring isle, and I am told that the flashing rays of the light pass across the roseate terns as they brood upon their eggs and light up their rosy breasts with striking and beautiful effect.

The watcher at a ternery is sometimes impressed by the sudden, silent flights of the terns out over the sea. The nesting site may be filled with cries, and with terns brooding eggs or feeding young, and suddenly, for no apparent reason, silence falls, and each bird flies, in complete silence and very swiftly, a little way out to sea, keeping close above the water in a compact flock. Then the birds return, still in silence, each settles beside its nest, and all is excitement and clamour once more. These seaward flights are periodic, and are made for no apparent reason. Kittiwake colonies sometimes behave in the same way.

The *common tern* nests, sometimes in vast colonies, along the coasts of Britain. It is also found, although not in colonies, along certain highland rivers, as the Aberdeenshire Dee, where, as a boy, I sometimes found the eggs on the broad shingle banks on the mid-reaches of that river.[1] The eggs were laid on the shingle, and as they harmonised perfectly with their surroundings, the only way to find them was to mark the sitting bird when she rose from them. On the coast, where these terns nest in colonies, there is no difficulty in locating the eggs: the birds here are very bold, and swoop at the head of anyone entering their nesting territory. Should a strange bird inadvertently fly over the colony the terns without hesitation attack it furiously and often force it to the ground. I have seen a cuckoo and a crow forced down to the sand for their lives (once the object of their hate has settled, terns do not attack it so fiercely), and light-keepers have told me that they have seen pigeons and other birds stabbed to death by terns.

The common tern and the Arctic tern closely resemble each other. The common tern is a bird of the more southerly districts, although it extends up the east coast of Scotland and nests plentifully on the Pentland Skerries, islands in the Pentland Firth between Caithness and Orkney. In the Hebrides and along the north-west coast of Scotland the Arctic tern is the species usually met with, and the range of the Arctic tern extends northward as far as Spitsbergen, where I have seen it nesting in small colonies beside the great walls of some glacier. The main points of difference between the common tern and

[1] On one Highland river the common tern nests over 1200 feet above sea level.

76 A Colony of Sandwich Terns

77 Puffins

78 A Pair of Kittiwakes with their Young

the Arctic tern are in the colour of the bill and in the cry. The common tern's bill is orange, tipped with black: the bill of the Arctic tern is crimson red from base to tip. The cry of the common tern has been likened to "kit, kit; keerie," and the alarm note to a long-drawn drawling "pee-e-rah." The call of the Arctic tern is more vigorous and hurried: a sharp "tchick, tchick, tchick." The alarm note or cry of anger as the bird swoops at an intruder is a fierce "kaah."

The *lesser* or *little tern* may be distinguished from common and Arctic terns by its small size and its white forehead (its cap is black). Its bill is yellow. The little tern is a most attractive bird: in appearance it is impish and gnome-like, and in its curious erratic flight it is like a will-o'-the-wisp. The little tern scrapes out its nesting hollow in sand or shingle, and often lines the hollow with dainty pieces of shell. Throughout the British Isles this tern nests sparingly, and in no districts is it numerous.

Unlike other British seagulls, which are described in another chapter, the *kittiwake* is a true bird of ocean. At the close of the nesting season the kittiwakes from Britain and those of Newfoundland often meet in mid-Atlantic, and above the stormy waters of mid-ocean these gentle birds pass the winter months.

The kittiwake receives its name from its cry, and a former name of this bird was cattiwike. It is the most delightful and inoffensive of British seagulls, and has so great a love for its home that if some disaster overtakes its brood, the parent birds will stand quietly, day after day, at their empty nest, finding happiness and solace in one another's company, until the time for the oceanward migration arrives. The kittiwake, besides being the most oceanic, is the tamest of British seagulls. There is an island in the Irish Sea where all the sea birds are carefully protected during the nesting season, and here is to be seen a little colony of kittiwakes on a low ledge of rock. There are hundreds, indeed thousands, of kittiwakes nesting on the higher rocks of the isle, but at this small, accessible colony the birds have become so tame that it is possible to walk up to them and to observe and photograph them without causing them to fly from their eggs or young. Kittiwake gulls are late nesters, and it is well on in June before the first of the young are hatched. Beautiful little balls of fluffy grey down, they are without fear during the early days of their lives. They are fed in a curious manner. The chick taps persistently on the parent's bill: the parent rising slightly on the nest opens its mouth and disgorges partially a half-digested fish. The fish is held, for a second or two only, at the top of the throat, where it can just be seen and reached by the kittiwake chick. The baby has time for no more than two or three quick pecks before the tempting food is swallowed once more. Again after a few minutes the baby taps feebly for food: again the fish is brought up for a few brief seconds. This goes on until the hunger of the young bird is satisfied. In the summer of 1936 I watched throughout a June night at this kittiwake colony, and during the hours around midnight the clamour of birds never died away. The high, impatient notes of kittiwakes mingled with the crowing of guillemots and the strong defiant calls of herring gulls, and as an accompaniment to this strange babel of sound the long, dreamy snore of a razorbill at long intervals drifted through the still night air. The greatest kittiwake colonies I have seen are on the sea cliffs of Unst, most northerly of the Shetland Isles. Here the kittiwakes have the unusual habit of forsaking the sea at least once each day in order to bathe in a fresh-water loch. Above this loch at any hour of daylight (and crofters living beside the loch tell me at any hour of the night also) a white cloud of kittiwakes may be seen hovering and alighting on the fresh water, there to bathe themselves with great eagerness and excitement. A continuous stream at any hour of the day may be seen flying in from the sea cliffs to the loch, and all the time this flight is being passed by an equally continuous stream of kittiwakes which, their bathing over, are flying back toward the sea and their nesting cliffs. To watch the kittiwakes on a summer day of sunshine bathing in the amber-coloured waters of this loch is a lovely sight, and the graceful, tern-like flight of the arriving and departing birds is always pleasant to see.

The *gannet* is the largest and most powerful in flight of British sea birds. In the year 1544 Turner wrote of the gannet as the goose of the bass: Willughby called it the soland goose. In Scotland at the present day it is almost always known as the solan: to the Gaelic-speaking fishermen of the west and north-west it is the *sulair*. It is no relation to the true geese. From the Land's End to John o' Groat's the gannet in spring, summer and autumn may be watched patrolling the seas: its flight is easy and powerful: on its well-tried wings it battles with each winter gale, for no gannet ever alights on land except at its own nesting rock, and its home is in the air or on the sea except during the nesting season.

The gannet appears to be on the increase, and this increase should be accelerated by the present-day immunity of the great St. Kilda colonies. So long as St. Kilda was inhabited the fowlers each summer scaled the gannet stacks twice or three times in the season. The first and second raids were for eggs, and upward of 1,500 of these were sometimes gathered at a time; the final raid took place in August, to kill the young gannets when they were plump and juicy and still unable to fly. Now that the people have left St. Kilda for new homes on the Scottish mainland the gannet population of St. Kilda should each year be increased by several thousand more birds than were fledged during the decades, perhaps centuries, when the fowlers made seasonal raids.

The gannet's aerial dive and plunge beneath the surface of the ocean after a fish is always spectacular. During the swoop the wings are usually driven strongly, in order to force down the bird the faster, so that the fish may have little time for escape before the dive. The gannet almost always swallows its fish beneath the surface, but on one occasion I watched a big flock of these birds diving for sand eels in shallow water and these solans reached the surface holding the fish in the powerful bill. Gannets are said to take their prey sometimes at a depth of twenty to thirty feet below the surface. It has not, I think, been proved to what depth a gannet can dive, but the deeper the bird submerges the more buoyantly it emerges on the surface after the dive. The dive is followed usually by a few seconds' rest and then the fisherman gives himself a shake and flies off low above the surface, to mount gradually and gracefully into the air and recommence fishing. Young gannets grow slowly, and they are upwards of three months old when they take the first flight from the nesting stack. Their parents have deserted them before the momentous first flight is made, and the pangs of hunger at last force them to take wing. The people of Lewis still make the perilous voyage to Sula Sgeir, and sometimes the even more hazardous passage to Stack Skerry, in open boats to bring back a supply of young gannets, which are salted down and used both as cattle and human food during the autumn and winter months.

The gannet is so fine and handsome a bird that it is pleasant to know it is increasing. Although its food is fish, almost all fishermen look upon it with favour. Since the Great War several gannet colonies have been established on Unst in Shetland, and a thriving one is now seen on the Muckle Flugga group, most northerly islets in Britain.

Three *petrels* skim the ocean waters of Britain and nest on her shores—the fulmar petrel, the stormy petrel, and the fork-tailed petrel. The *fulmar*, the largest of the three species, is sometimes known by fishermen as the St. Kilda gull. This bird is indeed much the same size as the common gull, but the thick neck, narrow, straight wings, and graceful gliding flight at once distinguish it from any gull. The flight of the fulmar when seen on a day of wind is one of the most beautiful things in the bird world, and when flying along a cliff face against a wind the birds sometimes move with motionless wings at a speed no greater than that of a walking man.

The fulmar lays one egg, on which it broods for eight weeks. The young bird is in the nesting hollow until the early part of September and, like the gannet, appears to take its first flight out over the great ocean unaccompanied by its parents. Since only one young bird is reared in the year it is surprising that the fulmar should be increasing everywhere on the coasts of Britain. Fifty years ago the fulmar's one British nesting station was St. Kilda. From St. Kilda it has spread, down the western seaboard to the south-west of Ireland, and along the east coast to Northumberland and Yorkshire, so that it will soon encircle Britain.

The *stormy petrel* has been likened to a long-winged, square-tailed house martin with a bat-like fluttering flight. This charming little petrel nests usually on uninhabited islands along the Atlantic seaboard of Britain. Except during the nesting season it lives far out on the ocean, beyond sight of land, and even during the nesting season the bird not on duty at the nest passes the hours of daylight (the stormy petrel is nocturnal) at sea, often a number of miles away.

The stormy petrel is one of the latest birds to nest in Britain, and it is usually the first days of July before the single glossy white egg is laid far down some hollow or in some rocky cavity. During the daylight hours the petrels are silent, but when at length the midsummer sun has set on the north-west horizon the air is filled with mysterious purring notes, which are difficult to locate. These notes come from beneath the surface of the

79 A Gannet fishing

80 A Great Skua at the Nest

81 A Fulmar brooding

ground and are the songs of the small petrels, now awakening with the coming of dusk and bestirring themselves. As the dusk deepens small bat-like figures may be seen to dart overhead in the uncertain light, and before a change of weather the petrels become filled with excitement and dash backwards and forwards, uttering ghostly cries which have been likened to the sound made by an asthmatic old gentleman clearing his throat.

It is not until mid-October that the young stormy petrels begin to leave the nesting crannies. In the blackness of an October night they scramble to the entrance of the burrow or hollow where their whole life has hitherto been spent. They listen, perhaps, to the wild song of the gale, and peer with their large and beautiful eyes out over the storm-vexed sea. Then, alone and unguarded by their parents, which have for some days deserted them, they spread their long wings, are caught up on the arms of the gale and fly out over the unknown sea, that is to be their future home.

The *fork-tailed*, or as it is sometimes called *Leach's petrel*, is slightly larger than the stormy petrel, and the forked tail distinguishes it from that bird. In Britain the fork-tailed petrel nests only on the most outlying Atlantic islands. I have seen the nest on the grassy slopes of Boreray of St. Kilda and on the surf-swept Flannan Islands, and there is also a considerable colony on Rona.

Shearwaters are ocean-loving birds. In British waters two species may be seen—the great shearwater, a regular wanderer from its breeding haunts in the southern hemisphere, and the Manx shearwater, so called because a colony of these birds formerly nested on the Isle of Man.[1] The Manx shearwater is also of the race of petrels; it glides with skilled flight just above the surface of the waves, shearing the water (as its name implies), and skilfully avoiding the overfalls of the waves. At sea it is sometimes seen in flight during the day, but over the land it is strictly nocturnal. It is not indeed until the darkest hour of the night that the shearwaters fly in from the sea to visit, and perhaps relieve, their brooding mates down in their nesting burrows. Shearwaters nest, often in large colonies, on grassy slopes near the sea. During the daylight hours there is nothing to show that hundreds, perhaps thousands, of birds are brooding beneath the ground, but at night sounds of indescribable confusion come from this hitherto silent nesting-place. One hears

[1] The Isle of Man colony was abandoned *circa* 1800, yet it is commemorated in the birds' name.

the crowing of pheasants, the hooting of owls, the screaming of cats—these, and other and more strange cries fall fast upon the night air. At times through the dusk the swift, wheeling flight of a shearwater is seen, but as soon, almost, as noticed the bird is swallowed up in the gloom.

Remarkable experiments in the "homing" of shearwaters have been made by the distinguished bird watcher and author, Mr. R. M. Lockley. A marked shearwater taken from the nest at Skokholm in the Irish Sea and liberated off the Faeroes was seen to fly, without hesitation, in the direction of the Irish Sea, and, still more remarkable, a shearwater despatched from Skokholm by air to Venice and released over the Adriatic was found not many days afterwards in its burrow on Skokholm.

The *skua gulls* are the pirates of the sea-bird world. There are in Britain two species of skua—the Arctic, sometimes called Richardson's skua, and the great skua or bonxie.

Both species depend for their food mainly on the efforts of other sea birds, which they chase so fiercely and relentlessly that they drop, or disgorge, their hard-earned catch of fish, and this the skua catches with dexterity in the air.

The *Arctic skua* is a dark, long-tailed bird, very graceful in flight. The species is dimorphic, and sometimes a male of the dark form will mate with a female of the pale form. This skua chases terns carrying home a sand eel for the family, and although the tern is a skilled flier, the Arctic skua in the end usually forces it to drop its catch. It also pursues puffins which are food-laden, and the puffin to escape its relentless enemy hurls itself into the sea and dives beneath the waves. But the Arctic skua can, on occasion, fish for itself, and is sometimes compelled to do so.

The slight nest is usually made in heather on boggy moorland, beside the sea, in the northern and western districts of Britain.

The *great skua*, a large, powerful bird, with short tail and strong heavy build, was on the verge of extinction not so many years ago. There were then a few pairs nesting in the Shetland Isles, on Foula and Unst. Thanks to the efforts of the family of Edmonston of Buness, who built a hut on the great skua's nesting hill and installed a watcher there, the great skua colony was saved, and subsequently greatly increased. The Royal Society for the Protection of Birds has carried on the good work of protection, and now on Hermaness a great skua colony of

82 A Guillemot carrying a fish

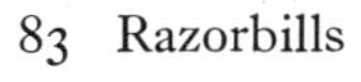

83 Razorbills

84 Shags (*above*) and Razorbills nesting together

85 A Cormorant feeding her Young

upwards of ninety pairs of birds has been established. The skuas of Hermaness appear to lead exemplary lives, but this cannot be said of the great skuas of Noss which seem to spend most of their time acting the hooligan. During the two hours which I watched at this comparatively new colony the skuas were continuously attacking passing gannets, and forcing them to disgorge the herring they were carrying home for the family. The outraged expression on the gannet's face was comical, but it was unable to shake off its assailant and was forced to disgorge its herring, which was caught by the tyrant skua in mid-air. One of these attacks was highly spectacular. A gannet, flying past at its best speed, was overtaken by a great skua, which actually alighted on the back of the flying solan and, maintaining its poise like a skilled horseman, by digs at the gannet's head and neck compelled the terrified bird to deliver up its herring. A few minutes later I came across a great skua murdering a kittiwake, eating into the back of the victim's neck as a stoat might behave with a rabbit. Even when the motor boat in which I was a passenger approached it, the skua was reluctant to leave its dying victim.

The *cormorant* and the shag are distant cousins of the gannet. They are expert fishers, and both nest commonly in Britain, but the shag is a bird mainly of the Atlantic seaboard, and the cormorant of the east. The cormorant is the larger of the two, and may be distinguished from the shag by the white chin and throat and also, in the breeding plumage, by the conspicuous white thigh spots. The cormorant is a much shyer bird than the shag, perhaps partly because it is shot at sight wherever the preserving of fish is attempted. There is no doubt that the cormorant is most destructive to fish of all kinds, and if a cormorant is seen fishing and diving in a pool of a river the human angler may as well go elsewhere that day.

The *shag*, on the other hand, fishes almost always in the sea, and because of its smaller size is less destructive. In the nesting season the shag assumes a conspicuous crest, which is often held erect, giving the bird the appearance of a schoolboy with unbrushed hair. Shags nest in colonies, and show great bravery in the defence of eggs and young. Some of the birds can scarcely be induced to leave their nests, and lunge forward at the human disturber of their peace, at the same time uttering fearsome shrieks, groans and grunts.

A friend of mine last year (1936) presented a young shag to

St. James's Park, London, and the bird became so tame that this absence of fear was the cause of its death. The ponds of the Park were being drained, and all the birds with the exception of the shag kept well clear of the workmen during the cleaning operations. But the shag, diving almost between the legs of one of the workmen, was carried by the suction down the overflow drain, and was drowned before it could be rescued.

The *chough*, a bird of the crow family, and in appearance like a slender crow, with red, curved bill and red legs, is now very rare in England and Scotland but in parts of western Ireland is still numerous.

In flight the chough is recognised by its delicate wing-beats and by the fact that the wing primary feathers are often widely separated. This attractive bird nests in sea caves. It was formerly plentiful on the west coast of Scotland and the Isles, but here is now almost extinct. Its high querulous cry carries far, but it is a shy, nervous bird, and rarely permits a near approach. Its haunts are in wild places. I once watched a family of full-grown choughs being fed by their parents on a lonely moor of a Hebridean island, while a few hundred yards away, at the foot of a high cliff, grey seals were baying mournfully and the great Atlantic rollers were thundering in, one after another on that calm summer's day when there was unrest only upon the ocean. There is an old Cornish legend that the spirit of King Arthur after death entered into a chough.

In olden times the name chough was applied to the jackdaw, and no doubt Chaucer was referring to the jackdaw when, in his "Parliament of Foules," he wrote of "the thief the chough."

The *rock dove* lives often with the chough on sea cliffs: indeed this bird never, so far as is known, nests inland. The rock dove can be distinguished from the stock dove by its white rump and under wing coverts. The flight of the rock dove is swift and sure. This bird is shy and is hard to approach. When Miss Frances Pitt was editing the *Romance of Nature* she found, if I remember rightly, that the only British bird which had never been photographed was the rock dove. This, of course, was not because of its rarity, but because its nesting-site is usually deep in the gloomy recesses of some Atlantic cave, where, even at a midsummer noon, there is twilight.

During the early spring of 1937 the authorities of the London parks decided to thin drastically the number of pigeons. Our daughter brought back with her to Skye a pair of blue pigeons taken in St. James's Park. The birds had their wings clipped, and it is only recently (the autumn of 1937) that they have recovered their full flight. They now fly as strongly as the local rock pigeons, with which they sometimes feed. One day recently I saw four pigeons with swift flight approach our stable. Two of them, our own birds, dropped to the stable roof; the two wild rock doves, obviously surprised at this behaviour, continued their flight. It is possible therefore that these London pigeons will be the means of taming some of the Skye rock doves!

The *whimbrel* is a regular passage migrant along our western coasts, and a few, a very few, pairs breed in the far north of Britain. With extreme regularity, whimbrels arrive in the west of Ireland and Scotland at the beginning of May, and because of this they are known in some districts as May birds. The whimbrel in appearance is like a small curlew, but is more confiding than the curlew, and may sometimes be closely approached. Its call note is a high-pitched whistle, "tetty tetty tetty tet." Most of the whimbrel which visit our coasts in late spring are on their way to Iceland, where the bird is very plentiful in summer. In the Hebrides these travellers sometimes remain until the end of May or even the opening days of June.

Sometimes on a grey December day, when the North Sea is angry and muddy and breaks far out in angry overfalls, a small dapper little bird may be seen swimming and diving close inshore. The bird is a *little auk*, a visitor from Novaya Zemlia or Jan Mayen, Franz Josef Land or Spitsbergen. Many thousands of little auks each year fly down to the North Sea from the Arctic; on the Atlantic waters of Britain they are less numerous. When repeated gales from east and north-east lash the North Sea to fury the little auks are sometimes in distress, and come close inshore to escape the fury of the waves. They are then almost without fear, and can be watched at very close quarters. Sometimes one of these birds may be seen nesting on the shore, actively preening its feathers, and then the bird-lover can be assured that this little auk's days are numbered, for the bird comes ashore only when its feathers are fouled by the waste oil of passing steamers. A friend of mine took an oiled little auk home, and in a few days the bird became quite tame, and would feed from the hand, but it is almost impossible to save a sea bird that has been poisoned by oil discharge, and this little auk lived only a week.

In Spitsbergen I have sat on a high and steep hill, and have listened to the music of innumerable little auks as they flew backwards and forwards high overhead, each one apparently attempting to whistle more loudly than its neighbour.

The rocky coasts of Britain are almost everywhere haunted by *rock pipits*. This friendly little bird is rather larger and of darker plumage than the meadow pipit, and lacks the white on the outer tail feathers. The nest is built on a rock close to the sea. The song is similar to the meadow pipit's song, but is, I think, less frequently uttered.

It is, perhaps, fitting to close this chapter with a few words on the *sea* or *white-tailed eagle*. It is a sad state of affairs that this great eagle should now be extinct as a nesting species in Britain, because as late as the middle of the last century it exceeded the golden eagle in numbers in the Isle of Skye, and nested in most of the Hebrides, Orkneys and Shetlands, besides on many sea cliffs of the western mainland. In Ireland it also bred, and on Lambay a rock where the sea eagle nested is still pointed out. I sometimes receive reports of the presence of sea eagles in different seaboard districts, but these reports are rarely correct, and usually refer to immature golden eagles, which have a certain amount of white on the tail. The sea eagle is a heavier and rather larger bird than the golden eagle, and lacks the dashing and alert appearance of the King of Birds.

The extinction of the white-tailed eagle is due largely to its fondness of carrion. Poisoned sheep were often placed in readiness for it by sheep farmers, who believed that it carried off their lambs, and the bird quickly became scarce, and has now disappeared from our shores, except when a wanderer from Scandinavia seeks our hospitality.

86 A Black-throated Diver on the Nest

87 A Heron with her Eggs

88 A Pair of Golden Eagles at the Eyrie: Male brooding Young, Female listening to Young cheeping

CHAPTER VII

Mountain Birds

It is difficult to separate moorland birds from birds of the high hills, but in this chapter I write of those birds which are found at or over the 3,000-feet level in the Scottish highlands.

Pride of place must be given to the King of Birds, the *golden eagle*, emblem of martial peoples, symbol of strength and beauty throughout the world; the "royal egle" of Chaucer that "with his sharpe look pierceth the sun."

Many poets have written of the eagle. Lord Tennyson gives a true and inspiring picture of the great bird:

> He clasps the crag with crooked hands:
> Close to the sun in lonely lands,
> Ring'd with the azure world, he stands.
>
> The wrinkled sea beneath him crawls:
> He watches from his mountain walls
> And like a thunderbolt he falls.

No poet, nor prose writer, has brought more vividly to the mind's eye a picture of the golden eagle. Not a word is superfluous, and the lines of the poem have a majestic clarity.

A different picture, but no less moving and strong, is drawn by Matthew Arnold:

> As when some hunter in the spring has found
> A breeding eagle sitting on her nest
> Upon the craggy isle of a hill lake
> And pierced her with an arrow as she rose,
> And follow'd her to find out where she fell
> Far off; anon her mate comes winging back
> From hunting, and a great way off descries
> His huddling young left sole; at that, he checks
> His pinion, and with short, uneasy sweeps
> Circles above his eyry, with loud screams
> Chiding his mate back to her nest; but she
> Lies dying, with the arrow in her side,
> In some far stony gorge out of his ken,
> A heap of fluttering feathers—never more
> Shall the lake glass her, flying over it;
> Never the black and dripping precipices
> Echo her stormy scream as she sails by.

In the western isles of Scotland there is a curious belief, widely held at the present day, that the eagle when he becomes old has difficulty in feeding because the upper mandible of the bill is growing over the lower. The eagle then breaks off the incurving portion of the bill on a rock, and when this has been done the youth of the bird is renewed. That the golden eagle is traditionally believed to live long is shown by the old highland adage:

> Thrice the life of a dog the life of a horse,
> Thrice the life of a horse the life of a man,
> Thrice the life of a man the life of a stag,
> Thrice the life of a stag the life of an eagle,
> Thrice the life of an eagle the life of an oak-tree.

There is no doubt that the golden eagle lives (if some untimely end does not overtake it) to a great age. It is, of course, a most difficult matter to obtain any proof of the eagle's age, but in the year 1845, according to the contemporary Press, a golden eagle was shot in France. A gold collar was observed round this eagle's neck, and on the collar was engraved:

> "Caucasus patria, Fulgor nomen, Badinski dominus mihi est 1750."[1]

It may be inferred that this eagle was used in the Caucasus for flying at game, and if the gold collar was placed on the eagle's neck as a young bird, its age when shot must have been ninety-five years.

My wife and I have watched the home life of the golden eagle from observation posts set up near eyries on trees or in rocks in different parts of the highlands, and a close and long acquaintance with this fine bird has increased our admiration for it. At one rock eyrie we watched for several years a pair of golden eagles from a hiding-post set up on a ledge of rock only a dozen feet from the nest. In time we became familiar with the male and female of this pair: we watched them, spring after spring, at such close quarters that their expressions, and even each gesture, became familiar and pleasing to us. I think that what most strongly impressed us was the keen glance of the eagles: we felt, as we crouched motionless in the heather hide, peering

[1] Caucasus, my Native Land, Lightning my Name, Badinski my Master 1750.

89 The Eyrie: a Golden Eagle bringing prey to the Family

From a Water-colour Sketch by J. C. Harrison

with one eye through a narrow peephole, that the flashing glance of the eagle on the eyrie was so penetrating that it must pierce the wall of our shelter.

On one occasion when I was in the eagle "hide" I noticed the female eagle on the eyrie becoming restless. Her restlessness increased, and she finally sprang into the air and flew away. I peered out carefully at the back of the hide in order, if possible, to ascertain the reason for her suspicions, and saw, fully a mile away, my wife and our collie dog walking up the glen. It gave me a feeling of satisfaction that I had been able to observe the eagle at the close range of twelve feet, yet the bird, so wild was her nature, had taken alarm at the sight of a human being a mile distant.

On one occasion my wife took an all-night watch in the hide, and was impressed by the fact that, although the eaglet cheeped continuously during the coldest hours of the night, the parent never actually settled on it to brood it, but crouched over it, shielding the "child" from the night dew but not from the night air. It was evident that this eagle believed in a spartan upbringing for the family. Before sunrise that morning a wandering blackbird which lived lower down the glen flew up, and, settling on the mountain-ash which grew near the eyrie, burst into a flood of joyous song. The eagle (eagles are heavy sleepers) had not yet awakened, and my wife told me that she was amused by the outraged expression of the great bird when unceremoniously aroused by the blackbird's song. The eagle glared at the blackbird which thereupon flew off to sing elsewhere; and the golden eagle again closed her eyes in sleep.

The golden eagle is the largest and most splendid of British birds, and I believe that it is holding its own in the Scottish highlands at the present day, despite the fact that it is shot and trapped whenever it unsuspectingly wanders to grouse moors. Although the golden eagle preys on grouse during that part of the spring when the eaglets are small, the harm it does on a grouse moor is rather in the number of birds it scares than the number it kills. Eagles take their prey usually on the ground, and indeed prefer hares and rabbits to grouse as food, and grouse, when they see an eagle, rise from the heather and fly aimlessly away in terror, usually at a considerable height. A small grouse moor may be cleared in this way of every one of its grouse for the time being, although the hunting eagles may not have taken, or even chased, a single bird. But even these misdeeds of the eagle do not excuse the horrible habit of certain keepers (encouraged or even ordered by their employers) of shooting the female eagle as she broods on the eyrie, despite the fact that in most highland counties the golden eagle is protected by law.

The *ptarmigan*, a true mountain dweller, is sometimes the golden eagle's prey. On the Cairngorm Hills I have frequently seen an eagle chasing, in play, a covey or pack of ptarmigan, and seeming to find satisfaction in the bewildered and aimless flight of the terrified birds.

Winter and summer ptarmigan remain on high ground. In the central highlands they rarely descend below the 2,000-feet level, and are found usually around the 3,000-feet level. In winter when the hills are in snow the ptarmigan in their white dress closely resemble the snowy wastes where they live, but should a thaw melt the snow the birds become so conspicuous that they can be seen from afar by their old enemies the fox and the golden eagle. Ptarmigan seem to realise this, and spend most of their time on some unmelted wreath of snow, venturing to the snow-free ground only to feed, and returning at once to the snow should an eagle appear. Snow has no terrors for ptarmigan so long as wind drifts the ridges bare and permits them to find their food—berries of hill plants or the tips of the young shoots. But when a prolonged snowstorm, unaccompanied by friendly wind, covers their feeding ridges deep in snow the ptarmigan are compelled to descend to the lower grounds. Their metabolism is adapted for low barometric pressures, and they are unhappy except on their high hills. It is indeed probable that, once they descend to the glens, they rarely return to the hills, but succumb to starvation and illness far from home.

I know of no more beautiful sight than a covey of ptarmigan feeding amid the winter snows in the slanting orange beams of the midwinter sun. They are unsullied as the virgin whiteness of their surroundings, and when they fly (which they do reluctantly) their white wings as they advance fearlessly beyond some vast precipice contrast in a beautiful and striking manner with the dark rock walls where snow finds no resting-place.

In late May the hen ptarmigan scrapes out a small hollow in the hill grass (ptarmigan nest usually above the heather line) and in it lays six to ten richly marked eggs not unlike those of her relative the red grouse. She is sometimes moulting at the time, and her white feathers form the lining of the nest. She broods very closely, perhaps more closely than any other British bird. On one occasion I removed an egg from beneath a sitting ptarmigan without causing her to leave the nest. I then very slowly and carefully lifted her from the eggs and held her gently in one hand. She made no attempt to escape, and when I set her again on the nest she at once brooded her eggs as before. A few days later when I climbed to the nest, which was placed 3,500 feet above sea-level, I found that she had successfully hatched her brood. It might be thought that this habit of brooding so closely might be to the disadvantage of a ptarmigan in exposing her to the sudden attacks of her enemy the hill fox. Nature wisely provides against this by removing the tell-tale scent from a brooding ptarmigan. My wife and I once had a collie dog who possessed a very keen scent and would scent grouse a hundred yards and more away. To see whether she would scent the ptarmigan which I lifted from the nest, I made her lie down on the ground about four feet from the bird. Although the breeze was blowing from the bird to the dog, the collie received no tell-tale scent and remained unaware of the ptarmigan's presence. It is, of course, true that the fox does sometimes catch a brooding ptarmigan, yet I think that on these occasions the fox wanders upon and sees, but does not scent, the bird.

The ptarmigan relies for protection on her admirable protective colouration, the fine golds and greys of her feathers resembling in a wonderful way the stones, lichens and mosses, amongst which she broods her eggs for three weeks.

Around the longest day of the year, when on the high hills there is no darkness at night but the long delaying sunset and afterglow imperceptibly merge with the first of the sunrise on the north-eastern horizon, the young ptarmigan broods are hatched. The ptarmigan chicks are able to run actively almost from the hour of their birth, as the following experience will show. One evening my wife and I were photographing a ptarmigan's nest in which the eggs showed no signs of hatching. The next morning when we climbed to the nest we found that the eggs had hatched, and that the young birds had run a considerable distance from the nest and were hiding in the grass and alpine plants.

The cock grouse is so devoted a parent to his young family

that it is remarkable that the cock ptarmigan, when his young are hatched, leaves his mate to bring up the family unaided. The cocks then (my observations have been made chiefly on the Cairngorm Mountains, which are the main stronghold of ptarmigan in Britain) form into packs, and fly up to the high plateaux where, at 4,000 feet, they lead a bachelor existence. When the families become full grown the male birds appear to return to their mates once more.

The word "ptarmigan" is from the Gaelic *tarmachan*. It is curious that the letter "p" should have crept into the word: it is said that this superfluous letter originated in the French language.

The *snow bunting*, a small bird slightly larger than the sparrow, is not uncommon in autumn and winter on the Scottish hills, and also along the north-east coasts of Scotland and England, but as a British-nesting species it is very rare and is found only on the highest Scottish hills where, in my experience, it is yearly decreasing. The male snow bunting in summer dress is a handsome bird in his black and white plumage and white crown. His song in his mountain fastness is wild and sweet, and carries far. In Spitsbergen I frequently saw the snow bunting's nest, but in the hills of the Scottish highlands, although I have searched for it for many years, I have never had the good fortune to find it. My nearest approach to success was at sunrise on a July morning, when, at a height of just under 4,000 feet on the Cairngorm Hills, a friend and I found a brood of snow buntings just out of the nest. We had walked all through the short summer night, and at four o'clock in the morning had reached the screes where we had seen a snow bunting the previous summer. We had not long to wait for a cheering sound. Beneath the thick mist blanket the clear whistling song of the snow bunting was heard, and hurrying in the direction of the song we saw a male snow bunting fly off, singing as he did so. The mist now lifted, and I was able to approach the bird as he stood on a large boulder, singing with scarcely a pause. This song consisted of six clear whistles, beginning in a low key and gradually rising. During his singing the bird moved about the boulder, and appeared to sing sometimes loudly, sometimes softly. Perhaps because of the different positions in which he stood, his song seemed to come now from one part of the hillside, now from another. After a time he flew down to the ground and began to feed, running actively about and apparently picking up small insects. He then flew a little way up the hill, and I saw a young snow bunting run up to him and stand expectantly, with open bill and quivering wings, imploring to be fed. The father fed the youngster, and then fed a second member of the brood which was near. I walked slowly up to this young snow bunting, and found it scarcely able to fly. I stood within five feet of it, and was able to take a number of photographs of it—the first photographs, I believe, ever taken in this country of a young snow bunting. The mother bird meanwhile flew up and endeavoured to persuade the youngster to fly away: she walked beside it and encouraged it with soft, twittering notes. She then fed it, regardless of my presence only a few feet away.

I have many times since then searched the hill, yet have never again seen snow buntings with their young here.

The *dotterel*[1] in Gaelic is usually termed *an t-amadan mointeach*, the fool of the peat moss. The name *dotterel* is also supposed to signify the foolish one. This bird has received names of contempt because of its absurd tameness. It appears to be unable to believe that human beings should wish it ill, and sometimes will brood with confidence on the eggs while the human onlooker is standing only a few feet away.

The dotterel at a distance resembles a miniature golden plover, but the white stripe over the eye, the white breast band and the chestnut lower breast and flanks serve to distinguish it from that bird. The dotterel is a summer visitor to Britain and perhaps nests highest of all British birds. I have not seen a nest lower than 3,000 feet above sea-level, and in June some years ago my wife and I watched a dotterel's nest at the great height of 4,000 feet above the sea. Here, even in fine June weather, the air was sometimes bitterly cold, for a few hundred yards south of the nesting ground was a great snowfield which almost filled a wild corrie, and when the wind blew from that quarter winter was in its breath. During the time we watched this nest the wind blew often with gale force, and the dotterel, when running round the nest in characteristic fashion at our approach, had often to crouch low, head to wind and legs firmly planted and wide apart, until the passing of some sudden and violent squall. The female dotterel is always the larger and more brightly coloured of the pair, and when she has laid the

[1] Not to be confused with the ringed plover, which is sometimes wrongly called the ringed dotterel.

three eggs—and very beautiful eggs they are—she ceases to take any apparent interest in them, and it is the male that broods on them and hatches them out.

We discovered the nest late one June evening when a cold and austere light lay over the plateau. The nest was a small cup scraped out in a tussock of wiry mountain grass and lined with dried leaves of the Alpine willow *salix herbacea*. For a dotterel, this bird was not tame: it was necessary to sit no nearer the nest than fifteen feet to watch him run back to the eggs. For some days the wind was so fierce that it was not possible to set up a hiding-tent on this exposed ground, but when at last the slackening wind permitted a hide to be erected, the dotterel paid no attention to it. Even when my wife and I went into the hide together, and conversed not more than twelve feet from the sitting bird, he ignored our conversation, and even dozed on the eggs. He had now been brooding a considerable time and was becoming thoroughly bored with this monotonous occupation. His wife, so far as we could see, gave him no encouragement, nor did she even come near him, and he often flew off the eggs to feed on the spiders and beetles which, even in cold weather, were plentiful on the plateau. On June 27th, a lovely still day of soft lights and shades and very clear air, we were early at the plateau. When we reached the nest we found that two of the eggs had already hatched and that one of the chicks was crouching on the ground about a foot from the nest. The father dotterel brooded the family with obvious pleasure, and when a pair of strange dotterel in their feeding incautiously approached the nest, he rushed at them with feathers ruffled and fiercely drove them away. By noon both chicks could run actively, and made small periodic excursions out of the nest, but returned at once obediently if their father called them. The third egg was addled, and when the chicks strayed farther afield, the father dotterel was torn between his desire to follow them and to brood the unresponsive egg. Several times he returned to the egg, brooding it for a few seconds and listening intently for the tapping of a young bird's beak within. But no sound rewarded him, and then he hurried after the two straying chicks and finally abandoned the egg. That day we made the interesting discovery that young dotterel leave the nest and run actively before their eyes are open. When last we saw the dotterel he was brooding the family beside a cushion of *silene acaulis*, the rosy petals of

90 A Male Dotterel with his newly hatched Young

91 A Ptarmigan

92 Grey Geese

which formed an island of glowing colour on that barren, windswept plateau on the roof of Scotland.

I think that of all our rare highland birds the dotterel is in most danger of extinction. Its absurd tameness—Bengt Berg photographed a dotterel brooding its eggs placed in his hand—renders its eggs an easy prize for collectors, and in these days of fast cars and excellent highland main roads it is possible to leave London by car one evening and be at the nesting ground of the dotterel before noon the next day.

I would earnestly appeal to bird lovers to do all in their power to retard the extinction of what is one of the most delightful and most confiding of British birds.

CHAPTER VIII

Wild Geese

THERE is no more majestic sight in the bird world than a skein of wild geese as they fly, unhurriedly yet swiftly, beneath a wine-coloured winter's sky. Their flight may be in the form of a chevron, or again in a long straight line. Rhythmic undulations pass through the skein, and the illusion is sometimes given of a pennon suspended miraculously in the heavens and slowly waving in the breeze. Geese are wise birds—there are few wiser—and, knowing man to be their enemy, they are ever on the alert against his coming. When feeding, wild geese always post a sentinel, and the sentinel is fully aware of his responsibility. Watch a flock of barnacle geese feeding, some fine day of April, on a grassy Atlantic isle. The shooting season is over, yet the birds are taking no chances, and while his fellows browse on the young grass with quick, eager movements, the sentinel, a lonely figure, stands on the crown of the isle, looking this way and that, now across the sea, now over the distant land, where he may see men, no larger than flies, walking or working in the fields.

Six species of wild geese commonly pass the winter in Britain. They are the *grey lag goose*, the *pink-footed goose*, the *bean goose*, the *brent goose*, the *barnacle goose*, and the *white-fronted goose*. Of the six, the only British-nesting species is the *grey lag*, and even the grey lag as a nester is a rare bird, and is confined to the Outer Hebrides and a few remote districts along the north-west mainland coast of Scotland. The grey lag is largest of British geese, and its wariness is not lost during the nesting season. I believe the grey lag is one of the very few birds which have a keen sense of smell when brooding. Almost all British birds rely on keen sight, but I am inclined to think that the grey lag when brooding detects danger by scent as well as by sight. Yet hand-reared grey lags, taken from the nest as eggs and hatched under a hen, sometimes become very tame, and an acquaintance of mine had a goose which used to fly away to the feeding grounds during the day, but returned home each evening. The grey lag is one of the so-called grey geese. The pink-footed goose, the bean goose, and the white-fronted goose, are all classed as grey geese. Grey geese are all land-feeders, and resort to the seashore only to sleep or to escape danger.

The Ross Links, a lonely and primitive part of the Northumbrian coast, which, it may be remembered, narrowly escaped in 1936 being made a bombing station for service aeroplanes, is a favourite winter and early spring haunt of three species of grey geese—the grey lag, the bean, and the pink-footed goose, and sometimes, on the same field of stubble or grass near the Links, the three species may be seen feeding together.

One spring day, when the daffodils were already in blossom in the farmer's garden, and the lapwings were wheeling madly through the air, I visited this haunt of grey geese. These birds, nesting far within the Arctic Circle, are in no hurry to fly north in spring, and remain here usually until early May. As I was watching courting lapwings, a gaggle of some forty grey geese, flying in from the east, alighted in a field near me and at once began to feed on the young grass. As wild geese always do when they alight on new ground, these birds sometimes interrupted their feeding to look round alertly, lest danger should overtake them, and it was interesting to see that they fed as readily when standing down-wind as when facing the breeze. Most birds feed only up-wind, as they do not like to have their feathers ruffled. For forty minutes the geese, without ceasing, grazed on the succulent grass, then walked across to a pool of water which lay on the field—the result of a recent storm—and drank long and eagerly: they then resumed their feeding. An hour and a half after they had arrived, sixteen out of the forty were either resting or asleep, and a little later one or two of the geese walked to the pool to bathe, throwing the water over their backs and forcing it under their wings. I expected that the geese would rest awhile after so prolonged a spell of feeding, but after a few minutes, those birds which were asleep or resting stretched wings and feet, and began to feed once more. But alarm seized the assembly, for no apparent reason, and the geese took wing for the neighbouring Fenham Slakes, where they alighted at the edge of the tide, and some of the birds fell asleep—a sleep which was interrupted by the fast-flowing tide. At first the geese endeavoured to avoid the encroaching water by walking away from it, but they seemed to decide that this was unsatisfactory, and turning to the tide, they allowed themselves to be overtaken, and dipped down to feel the cool caress of the sea, and swam close together a short distance off-shore.

As I watched the geese, many larks sang on high and a redshank flew from a boggy field almost vertically into the clear air, and sank again earthward on drooping wings, all the while uttering his flute-like song.

It is not easy to distinguish between the three species of grey geese—the grey lag, the pink-foot and the bean—which haunt the Ross Links. If the light is clear, and the observer is armed with a good glass, the appearance of the upper mandible of the bill is a sure guide between grey lag and the two other species. In the grey lag goose the upper mandible is tipped with white; in the pink-footed and the bean with black. The bean goose is hard to distinguish from the pink-footed goose, but it is usually the larger of the two, and the bill is thicker and longer. Abel Chapman, a noted hunter and observer of geese, was of the opinion that the only sure means of distinguishing between the bean and the pink-footed goose was the size of the bill. The pink-footed goose had, he said, a tiny and delicately shaped bill resembling the bill of the brent goose rather than of a grey goose.

The *pink-footed goose* nests in the far north. In a lonely valley of Spitsbergen, where the midnight sun shone cold and clear, I saw my first pink-foot's nest, on a little knoll from which the snow had only recently melted. On the same knoll were the remains of a number of old nests of (I imagine) the same pair of geese, and it is quite possible that among the birds I had sometimes watched feeding on the Ross Links was the pair which I had seen nesting up that lonely Spitsbergen glen. The distance from Northumberland to Spitsbergen may be reckoned as a good 1,500 miles—this means a 3,000-miles flight by the geese each year between nesting valley and winter haunt. But even that long flight is as nothing to the migration of the Arctic tern, which nests as far north as Spitsbergen and in winter has been seen on the ice floes of the Antarctic, having flown almost from pole to pole in search, we may perhaps assume, of the perpetual daylight of a polar summer.

White-fronted geese prefer as winter quarters rough, boggy moors rather than fields, but at Holkham, in Norfolk, they sometimes join the other grey geese which feed here in winter. One of their Scottish haunts is beside a small tarn on rough boggy ground near the Minch. Here are deep peat hags, and the stumps of ancient trees, blackened by the peat. One December afternoon I reached the neighbourhood of the lochan before dusk and, peering cautiously round a large stone, I saw a number of white-fronts standing, asleep, on a rock which rose from the water near the centre of the tarn. After a time they awakened one by one, jumped down into the water, and began to feed on aquatic weed in the shallows. This did not seem to please them, for they soon left it and landed on the shore, walking in single file along the bank and plucking at the brown grasses that fringed the shore. But all the time one of the geese stood on guard, an alert figure with a white forehead that was clear against the dark background.

The handsome *barnacle goose* received its name from a curious belief that the bird began its life as a barnacle, floating, head down, from water-logged wreckage in the ocean. This strange belief was widespread: indeed all the early naturalists credited it. Gerard in his *Herbal* (1597) states that "as it [the barnacle gosling] groweth greater, it openeth the shell by degrees till at length it is all come forth and hangeth only by the bill: in short space after, it cometh to full maturitie and falleth into the sea, where it gathereth feathers."

The earliest writer who believed that the barnacle goose began life as a barnacle was, so far as is known, Giraldus Cambrensis, whose day was in the late twelfth century. But the belief long persisted in certain out-of-the-way districts of the west, and, like the fable of the horsehair which gives birth to an elver when placed in water, may linger here and there until the present day. This remarkable superstition could not have taken root if eggs of the barnacle goose had been seen, but since this goose nests only in the far north—in Greenland, Spitsbergen and Franz Josef Land—the eggs were unknown.

For a goose, the nesting site of this bird is unusual. It was eleven o'clock on an evening of late June when I saw for the first time the nesting haunt of barnacle geese in Spitsbergen. The sun, even at this late hour, shone brightly in the northern sky and the air was crisp and invigorating. I reached a narrow glen with buttresses of rock on either side. At the head of the glen was a great glacier, and beyond the glacier a high hill on which snow still lay, deep and unbroken. Through the glen flowed a river muddy with the melting snow which had disappeared from the ground only a few days before. The frost had left the earth like a sponge, so that my feet sank deep into mud and water at each step: the scanty Arctic vegetation was brown and had scarcely begun to awaken. On the west side of the glen, perhaps a mile from the sea, rose buttresses of rock in tiers, one above the other, and here thousands upon thousands of little auks were nesting or were flying in a continuous stream through the air, and were producing a pandemonium of whistling cries. Upon the buttresses perhaps a dozen pairs of barnacle geese were nesting. Some of the geese when disturbed rose into the air and flew backwards and forwards across the glen calling with deep honking cries which, in Britain, are associated with mist-shrouded islands of the Atlantic seaboard. A goose after a time flew to the top of one of the buttresses and alighted, apparently on a nest. The midnight hour was now approaching: the air was very still and the west slopes of the glen were in deep shade, although the midnight sun shone with mystic light on the opposite face and on the hills, blue and ethereal where the snow had left them.

I climbed the west side of the glen to a height of 1,000 feet above sea-level, making my way over loose and sharp screes where cock snow buntings, handsome in their black and white plumage, silently flew. Around and above me thousands of little auks were nesting—in crannies among the rocks, on the ground in holes, beneath boulders. Those not brooding the single egg the species lay, were either standing about on the rocks or were flying backwards and forwards, uttering their high-pitched cries. Sometimes they flew above the shaded slope into the light of the midnight sun, and at once their plumage changed to silver in the low sun's rays. Tirelessly these little auks swept round in great circles, the birds keeping in companies, and each company flying close to that part of the rock where, I imagined, their mates were brooding. In the glen below glaucous gulls were calling and snow buntings twittering. The nest of the barnacle goose was placed on the top of the buttress where the bird had alighted. It was a shallow nest, lined with a little down, and the eggs were large and shiny.

A few days later, in the same glen, I saw another barnacle goose's nest. I was resting beside a great boulder, enjoying the Arctic sunshine, when a barnacle goose crossed one of the buttresses above me with leisurely, powerful flight and alighted on a ledge of a perpendicular rock face. Here the bird stood, each feather distinct through the field of my telescope, and then I suddenly saw a second goose, brooding on a nest a few feet away. After a time the brooding goose rose on her nest, and arranged the down more to her liking, and I could see her black gorget and white breast and cheeks. This nesting site was one which, in Britain, a raven or a peregrine falcon might have chosen.

Plant life in the Arctic, growing fast in the continuous daylight, springs up more quickly in Spitsbergen than in Britain, and already in places the hillside was creamy white with the buds and flowers of *dryas octopetala* and purple with the lowly blooms of *saxifraga oppositifolia*. In these beautiful surroundings the barnacle goslings are hatched: how they make their way from the cliffs, through or over the screes to the glen beneath and thence to the sea, is a mystery.

It is late autumn when these Arctic-nesting geese reach Britain. After rearing their broods in the Arctic the geese moult and become flightless for a time. Then their new wing feathers grow and the birds are now ready for their long overseas flight to Britain. One autumn morning the barnacle geese are seen, standing motionless, tier upon tier, on the isle where they will remain throughout the winter. Their actual arrival is rarely witnessed, but it is noticed that when they arrive they are unreasonably filled with alarms and are almost impossible to approach. Their black and white plumage makes them curiously like barnacles when they are seen from a distance clustered on a rock beside the tide, and indeed it might be thought that the name "barnacle goose" had been given them because of this resemblance. Their flight is graceful, whether they hang almost motionless on the breeze or drift, as it seems, backwards and forwards above the sea that sparkles beneath them in the low autumn sun. As they fly, their voices carry across the ocean—wild music in harmony with the rush of the seas that break mightily on their island rocks. Sometimes the geese alight on the sea when alarmed, but rarely remain long on the waves, and as they rise shake the salt water in spray from their handsome feathers.

The *brent* is the smallest British goose, and weighs less than half the grey lag. It is the only true marine goose in Britain, frequenting, during its stay with us, the salt, though comparatively calm water, of river estuaries and land-locked bays. Brents in winter live a communal life, and thousands of birds may be present at some favoured haunt. When a shore gunner's shot sends the brents into the air together the sound of their wings is like the surge of a heavy sea, and their voices like a pack of hounds in full cry.

On Moffen Island, a low isle in 80° N. latitude off the Spitsbergen coast, I saw during a few hours three nests of brent geese, and one of the nests was on the shingle, in a site which in Britain might have been chosen by an oyster catcher. The eggs, white and shiny, lay on a thin layer of down, plucked from the bird's own breast. The brent goose nests mainly on islands in the Arctic; it is reluctant to lay on the mainland because the Arctic fox, which fears the pink-footed goose because of its strength and size, does not hesitate to attack the smaller brent.

But even the pink-foot is glad to nest in the sanctuary of some cliff, as I saw one night on the desolate, snow-clad isle of Prince Charles Foreland. It was midnight, and mist shrouded the hills and at times dropped to the sea itself as I walked below gloomy cliffs and saw large numbers of pink-footed geese fly out to sea. Prince Charles Foreland is uninhabited, and thus it might be thought that the geese here would show little fear of man, but, perhaps because of unpleasant experiences in winter in the south, they remain alert and wary. On ledges of the cliff pink-footed geese were nesting, and one pair were particularly anxious when they left the nesting ledge where four tiny goslings stood up in the nest and began to cheep.

CHAPTER IX

Waders in Autumn and Winter on British Coasts

In this chapter a short description will be given of some of the more numerous waders which do not nest in Britain but which visit us each autumn and winter, either to remain awhile with us on their passage to more southerly lands or to spend the winter months on our shores.

Some of these waders live a communal life during winter, and these birds are most inspiring to watch as they wheel, dip and glide as a single individual: it has indeed been suggested that they are guided by a "group soul."

Of the autumn migrants which spend a short time with us after their journey from the Arctic perhaps the most interesting is the *sanderling*, an active bird slightly larger, and much whiter, than the dunlin. Sanderlings are often seen in September and October haunting low sandy shores on which, in certain lights, they look as white as seagulls, but of course much smaller.

It is a peculiarity of sanderlings that they feed mainly at or near high tide, and not, like most waders, towards low water. They follow up each succeeding wave as it recedes from the sandy shore, to pick up sandhoppers and other sea life that the wave has deposited high and dry. Sometimes the sanderlings wade thigh-deep into the sea, and when a wave threatens to overwhelm them they rise on graceful wings with a quick movement out of reach of the sea. One day I watched a flock of sanderlings feeding with incredible speed at the edge of the waves, and when I walked down to the margin of the tide I found the sand here covered with countless small amber-coloured worms or larvae. So delicate were these creatures that when I placed some of them on my finger and held them a few minutes exposed to the air they dried up and lost their form.

When feeding, the black legs and bills of a flock of sanderlings contrast pleasingly with their white under-plumage, and in flight the white wing bar is noticeable.

The *knot*, so named because King Canute loved, above all

birds, a knot for his dinner, spends the months of winter on our coasts. It is seen usually in great flocks, and these flocks, moving over the sea or along the coast, travel very fast and in close formation, so that each bird seems almost to touch its neighbour. The knot is considerably larger than the dunlin and sanderling, and is short of leg and plump of form. In early summer, before the knot leaves for its nesting haunts in the far north, it assumes a plumage in which dull red predominates, and is then a bird of great beauty.

Like the knot, the *turnstone* is a bird of the Arctic, and remains on our coasts throughout the winter. It may be recognised by its red legs and tortoise-shell plumage. The turnstone has received its name because of its habit of turning over stones, shells and seaweed in its energetic search for food.

A pair of turnstones which I observed and photographed from a hiding-tent on a low island of Liefde Bay, in north Spitsbergen, were very tame. It was a grey misty morning in the first week of July when I set up my hide beside the turnstone's nest, and almost before I had focused the camera the male turnstone returned to the nest, as a few flakes of wet snow fell. In the grey light he was a strikingly handsome bird. The crown of his head, with the exception of a few small black feathers, was white; near each ear was a small dark patch. Round his neck, like an evening tie, was a band of black feathers; his gorget was black and his breast white. After brooding the eggs for a time the turnstone was relieved by his mate. The "change-over" was preceded by a charming little incident. The male, rising from the nest, walked slowly away and as he walked he stooped and picked up small stones and threw them over his back in the direction of the eggs. I then saw that the hen bird, as she approached the eggs, was doing exactly the same thing. During the female turnstone's spell on the eggs an Arctic tern, flying over the island, caught sight of her and swooped angrily at her, uttering a harsh cry of rage, but, without actually touching her, flew on.

The weather cleared, and from the hide I was able to look out across the fjord to the conical mountains to the south. The colouring of these hills was remarkable. One peak was dull red and gave the illusion that the sun was shining upon it: near it was a hill which, at a distance, appeared pale green. Around some of the hills thin, ethereal mist lay—a mist which did not hide the mountains but rendered their outline soft and delicate. In Britain we never see mists so delicate and thin as these of the Arctic; they resemble passing showers of fine snow.

The *purple sandpiper*, which also winters in Britain, and is perhaps the tamest shore bird we have, was nesting on the tundra of Spitsbergen near the turnstones. It is a sober-coloured bird and the plumage has a purple gloss on the upper parts, hence the bird's name. In winter the purple sandpiper haunts low, rocky coasts where on occasion it can be approached very closely. I have sometimes at ebb-tide watched it, apparently feeding on barnacles on the wet rocks, and it is an expert at avoiding the sudden onset of a wave. One mild winter morning recently when I was having my before-breakfast swim in the Isle of Skye, a purple sandpiper alighted on a low rock near me, and as I swam towards it the bird paid no attention to me and I almost put my hand on it before it flew: it perhaps thought I was a friendly seal. In Spitsbergen the purple sandpiper is not uncommon in summer. The first nest which I saw was beside a log of driftwood and the four eggs lay on a dry bed of the leaves of *salix polaris*. Another nest was on the moss of the tundra. Here the male bird was brooding and when disturbed he fluttered round, feigning injury in order to distract the attention of his presumed enemy from the eggs. His shrill cries of alarm soon brought his mate on the scene, and when she arrived he became still more excited, fluttering, and apparently rolling, over the ground with feathers dishevelled as though grievously injured. Despite his excitement his mate walked to, and settled down on, the eggs with little fear.

At a nest which I found later, I made the interesting discovery that the bird not in charge of the young brood will on occasion sham injury and feign terror, although the young may be some distance away and in no danger of discovery. But the shamming under these conditions is less realistic, and the bird will suddenly cease its antics and feed unconcernedly awhile, then, as though half-unconsciously, again feign acute distress.

In some parts of Spitsbergen the nesting season of the purple sandpiper must be very late. On July 1st, on Prince Charles Foreland, the snow lay deep and unbroken above the tide-mark, and the purple sandpipers could not make a start with their nesting, but were obliged to feed on the narrow strip of snow-free ground immediately above the sea.

The *bar-tailed godwit*, a long-legged bird of slender appearance with long bill slightly curved upward, is numerous on low sandy shores and river estuaries in winter. This species is almost always seen in flocks, and the birds are remarkable for their graceful and delicate flight, often on drooping wings. By the flight alone godwit and knot are readily distinguished. There is nothing ornamental in the flight of the knot—it is strong and swift and serviceable—but there is pure poetry in the flight of a large flock of godwits. These godwits nest on Siberian tundras, and each year must traverse a great distance, over sea and land, between summer quarters and winter haunts.

The *black-tailed godwit* in flight can be distinguished from the bar-tailed godwit by the broad white wing bar, very striking when the bird flies into the dark and stormy sky. This godwit is a passage migrant, and is seen singly more often than in flocks: a hundred years ago it nested in England, and the last certain record of a nest was from Norfolk, in 1847.

This chapter will close with a few words on the *grey plover*, a bird rather larger than the golden plover, and silver, not golden, on the upper parts.

Unlike the golden plover, which remains flocked during winter, the grey plover is usually found either singly, or in small companies consorting with dunlin flocks and feeding with these small waders, through which it stalks like a giant. This plover nests in Siberia, and in summer is strikingly handsome, with more black about its plumage than the golden plover.

Another point of difference, in winter, between the two plovers is that the golden plover feeds near, but rarely on, the shore, and the grey plover feeds almost always on wet sands or mud flats.

Besides the waders I have written on, there are other waders, such as dunlin, redshank, and greenshank, which I have described elsewhere, and also rare visitors, as the little stint and the curlew sandpiper, which there is space merely to mention.

93 A Turnstone

94 Sanderlings

95 Black-headed Gulls against a Winter Seascape

CHAPTER X

British Seagulls with Inland Habits

It is often said that British seagulls are changing their habits, that they are more land birds than they used to be. It is difficult to know how much truth there is in this assertion, but there is no doubt that the kittiwake (which I have described in the chapter on sea birds) is the only British seagull which spends its life on the sea.

Take, for example, the *black-headed gull:* this gull is seen during the greater part of the year inland. It may nest fifty miles from the sea, and in winter may frequent reaches of inland rivers such as the Thames. The black-headed gull is, of all seagulls, the most familiar to Londoners. Each autumn thousands of these birds arrive at the London parks, and any day up to mid-March these gulls may be seen circling over St. James's Park, Hyde Park and the Serpentine, or standing on the banks of the lakes. They receive so friendly a welcome from their human friends that they are very naturally pleased to remain in the pleasant surroundings, where one human admirer vies with another in offering them food of many kinds. Of all these foods, suet, or fat, or bacon is their favourite. When feeding the gulls of St. James's Park on bacon I have had a black-headed gull repeatedly perch and stand on my head, while others rested for a moment on my outstretched hand. There was a curiously gentle and caressing feeling when they stood on my hand; a strange sensation that these truly wild birds which at the coming of spring flight across the North Sea to their nesting grounds in lands near, or on the Baltic, should have so little fear of their hereditary enemy, man.

The black, or more correctly the dark chocolate-brown head which the black-headed gull assumes for the nesting season (in winter there is only a small dark spot on either side of the head) is well known, and the red bill and feet are also distinguishing features of this gull, which is the farmer's friend to the extent that it eats large numbers of the wireworm grub of the daddy-long-legs or crane-fly, so destructive to young oats. But its egg-stealing habits are not, I think, sufficiently widely known, and during a dry season, when its natural food is scarce, the black-headed gull ranges far and wide, even to the haunts of the ptarmigan, in search of eggs or unprotected young birds. The gulls sometimes nest on grouse moors in large colonies.

The *common gull* is a rather larger bird than the black-headed gull, and its wings are less narrow. The white area of feathers near the wing tip is another distinguishing feature.

Many common gulls nest on grassy islands along our western seaboard, but others breed in small colonies on lochs and tarns far inland, and sometimes over 3,000 feet above sea-level, where many ptarmigan eggs are stolen and can be seen lying, sucked, in the shallow waters of the gulls' loch.

The name "common" when applied to this gull is scarcely correct, for the black-headed gull is more common by far in Britain. The common gull nests in Scotland, but very rarely in England, to which country it is a winter visitor.

The *herring gull* is like an overgrown common gull, and is more marine in its habits than the latter bird: it is indeed a shore gull in most districts, haunting fishing harbours throughout the year and nesting usually on sea-cliffs and less frequently on grassy islands. Like the common gull, it has a pale grey back.

The *lesser black-backed gull*, which is similar in size to the herring gull, is likely to be confused only with the *greater black-backed gull*; it can be distinguished from that species by its smaller size, and its dark slate-grey rather than black upper parts. It is not generally known that the lesser black-backed gull is a summer visitor to the British Isles, and that it winters off the coasts of Spain, Portugal and Africa. Of recent years the Scandinavian lesser black-backed gull has been separated from the British species, the difference being that it has a black and not a slate-grey mantle. It is probable that the many hundreds of lesser black-backed gulls which pass north-east above the Spey valley in April and early May each year belong to this species: the birds travel in small flocks, and day after day are seen to be flying towards the north-east, sometimes in the teeth of the snow squalls which often sweep this upland valley in April. The greater black-backed gull, a powerful, cunning bird, has been known to attack full-grown grouse and, as I have mentioned elsewhere in this work, kills many puffins, shearwaters and stormy petrels. This great gull is also fond of carrion, and a dead sheep lying by the shore is quickly

96 Black-headed Gulls in their Summer Plumage

97 A Lesser Black-backed Gull at the Nest

98 A Greater Black-backed Gull with her Young

99 A Common Gull brooding

100 A Herring Gull calling

101 Mallard

102 A Sheldrake guarding the Family

discovered and feasted upon. During the winter greater black-backed gulls fly up the rivers of the highlands to feed upon the salmon which succumb after the spawning season. With the greater black-backs are sometimes seen one or two glaucous gulls, large white gulls from the Arctic which occasionally fly south in winter to Britain and are fond of a dead or dying salmon. When fishing on the Aberdeenshire Dee on the opening day of the salmon angling season in February I once saw, haunting the same pool, greater black-backed and glaucous gulls, and noticed how annoyed they were at being disturbed and how reluctant they seemed to move from their feeding-place.

CHAPTER XI

British Ducks

In a single chapter it is impossible to describe at all fully the various ducks found in Britain: extensive books have been written on this subject alone. Ducks, with their eclipse plumages after the summer moult, are very difficult to identify, and they require specialised study.

The *sheld-duck*, a marine duck which haunts river estuaries, sand-dunes and mud flats, has the carriage, and to some extent the flight of a goose, but if a close view is obtained of the bird the bright red bill and the chestnut band on the breast are noticeable. Sheld-ducks are deliberate, unhurried birds, and are not really wary except where they are disturbed or shot. They sometimes are seen in large flocks at the feeding grounds of brent geese, but feed apart from the geese, and permit of a nearer approach. In spring the sheld-duck chooses a rabbit burrow on the sand-dunes as a nesting site, and there broods in darkness until the ducklings are hatched and she leads them across the sands to the sea. Sheld-ducks are excellent mothers, and it is no uncommon sight to see a dozen well-grown ducklings following their parent over the sand and rocks into the sea, and swimming after her in a long line.

The *mallard* or common wild duck is distributed throughout the British Isles, and on occasion becomes very tame. Its relative the *gadwall* resembles it, but is rather smaller, rests higher on the water, and in flight the wings are more pointed. This duck nests in Norfolk and Suffolk, and, more recently, in certain counties of Scotland.

The *teal* is recognised at a glance because of its small size. Its flight is swift and slightly wavering, and it is altogether a most active little duck.

The *garganey*, sometimes called the summer teal, is distinguished from the common teal by the broad white eye stripe and pale blue shoulder. Its flight is even more rapid than the teal's flight, but is steadier and lacks the sudden turns and downward plunges. The garganey is a summer visitor to Britain, and nests chiefly in Norfolk and Suffolk.

The *widgeon* nests in Britain, but is best known as a winter visitor to our coasts, where thousands upon thousands of these birds assemble where the feeding is good. A favourite haunt of widgeon is the Ross Links in Northumberland. The widgeon here spend the daylight hours on the open sea where, a few hundred yards east of the line of breaking waves, they are secure from their enemies, the shore gunners. At night the widgeon fly in over the sand-dunes to the Fenham Slakes, where they feed on the marine grass—*zostera marina*. The swift flight of the widgeon as they make for the open sea at dawn, their high-pitched whistling cries, their characteristic formation —all these things are pleasant for the nature-lover to see and hear. The male widgeon is a handsome bird, and his gold forehead and crown and chestnut head and neck at once identify him. In flight the white shoulder patch of the male and the double white wing bar of the female are guides to identification. Widgeon nest on moorland lochs in the highlands, in long heather or rushes, often on an island. The species seems to be increasing and extending its range southward.

The *pintail* is perhaps the most graceful of all British wild ducks. In the Downpatrick marshes in Northern Ireland pintail and widgeon are to be seen any winter's day, and when the pintails rise into the air their flight is so graceful and delicate that even the widgeon in comparison appear heavy and clumsy.

The elongated tail feathers are very characteristic of the pintail in flight and also at rest on the water.

The *shoveller*, a duck with a bill enormously widened near the tip, is a bird of heavy build, walks low and "stooping," and swims low. These ducks used to arrive at the Fallodon ponds in autumn, and although they were strangers to the district they became so tame that they would walk up to Lord Grey and feed at his feet. As a nesting species the shoveller is increasing in Britain, and nests in England, Scotland and Ireland.

The *pochard* is known by its chestnut-red head and neck and black breast. In winter pochard may be seen swimming and diving assiduously in districts where they are unknown in summer. It may be because of the colour, but I have the impression of the pochard as a bird with an unusually deep head.

The *tufted duck* is one of the most delightful of British ducks, and the jaunty tuft, and white sides of the male (his plumage is otherwise black), are unmistakable. This duck becomes very tame if it is not alarmed, and at Fallodon tufted ducks used to come up to Lord Grey and pull his shoelaces if he disregarded their pleading looks for food.

The tufted duck is a bird mainly of the fresh water : the *scaup duck* at its winter haunts frequents usually salt water. The scaup has no crest, and the back of the male is lighter. The female scaup has a white band at the base of the bill.

The scaup is a rare nester in this country. In the Outer Hebrides some years ago I saw a scaup's nest on an island of a fresh-water loch. The male bird of this pair was a tufted duck.

The *goldeneye* is a handsome black and white duck, with a white patch beneath the eye. Like the scaup the goldeneye is chiefly a salt-water feeder in winter, and remains at sea even during heavy weather. These ducks are skilled divers, and in the sea feed mainly on shellfish.

The goldeneye has not been proved to nest in this country, although it is sometimes seen on highland lochs until late in May. Its nesting grounds are to the north of us, although in Iceland it is rare.

The *long-tailed duck*, called sometimes the sea pheasant, in my mind is associated with winter days in the Outer Hebrides and also with the coast of Northumbria. The long curled tail feathers, black and white plumage, and skilful and prolonged diving serve to identify this visitor from the Arctic. It is seen in winter at sea usually above a sandy bottom, and dives for shrimps and small crabs.[1] In Northumberland it is called by fishermen the pintail.

The *common eider*, a large heavy duck of the sea-coast and islands, nests in Scottish waters, and as far south as Coquet Island. On the Farne Islands in Northumberland there is a considerable colony, and the birds remain on that part of the coast throughout the year. Some of the fishermen of Seahouses, on the mainland over against the Farnes, have fed the eiders during the few past winters, and these birds have become so tame that they swim into the little harbour of Seahouses on the flood tide, and take the mussel bait offered them by their fishermen friends. Some of them, I believe, actually take food from the human hand, and tap on the side of a boat if its occupants are slow to offer them food. The eider drake is a very handsome bird. His crown is black, his upper parts white,

[1] In early November 1942 I saw a long-tailed drake diving repeatedly in a moorland loch in Sutherland. This is the first time I have seen the species on fresh-water in Scotland.

his breast pale rose-coloured, and on the sides of the head and neck are sea-green patches. At Fallodon Lord Grey had a tame eider drake which reached the age of twenty-one years, and in his old age used to court the mallard ducks, to the tolerant amusement of the drakes.

In Northumberland the eider is still known to fishermen as Cuthbert's duck, because of the tradition that St. Cuthbert, who had his cell on one of the Farnes, long ago tamed the eiders of the place; although they may not realise it, these fishermen are thus carrying on an age-old tradition.

The male *common scoter* is unmistakable. His plumage is unrelieved black, the only patch of colour being the yellow on the bill. The duck is brown, with grey cheeks. Scoters are sea birds except during the nesting season. They usually pass the winter in great flocks, so far off shore that they can be identified only through a powerful glass. They have a habit of rising from the water as individual birds, and taking short flights on fast-driven wings just above the water's surface, alighting again in the sea with a heavy splash. This duck nests in the highlands of Scotland and Ireland, but is nowhere numerous as a nesting species, and the great flocks seen at their winter haunts are mostly migrants from the north.

The *velvet scoter* is rather larger than the common scoter, and can be distinguished from it by the white wing bar, and also by the white mark which almost encircles the eye. It also is a visitor from the north, and does not nest with us.

The *merganser* family of ducks are distinguished by their saw-like "teeth," very sharp and directed slightly backwards. There are three British species—the goosander, the red-breasted merganser and the smew.

The *goosander* is the largest of the three. It is a handsome bird with green head, red bill, black back and white wings. The female has the head red-brown, and both male and female goosander have crests. As a nesting species the goosander is confined to the highlands of Scotland, where it makes its nest in a hollow tree, or beneath a stone, or in a hole on the steep bank of some rushing hill stream. The same nesting site is used year after year when the birds are not molested, but the goosander is unpopular in the highlands because of the number of salmon parr it devours, and the birds are trapped and the eggs destroyed in many districts. Baby goosanders have long and sharp claws, and my wife watched a family climb out of a deep hollow tree when only a few hours old, mounting a vertical smooth wall of wood about two feet deep without difficulty.

The *red-breasted merganser* resembles the goosander, but is considerably smaller, and nests not along mountain streams like the goosander but on the banks of Scottish rivers, and on islets on sea lochs on the west coast. The goosander lays her eggs in April: it is June before the red-breasted merganser nests.

The *smew* is a scarce winter visitor to British waters. The drake is a most handsome bird, almost white in plumage, with black on the wings and back. It is the smallest of the "saw-bill" family, and is seen usually on salt water, chiefly on the east coast of Britain. The smew, like the other members of the "saw-bill" family, is an expert diver and swimmer.

The nesting haunts of the smew are far north—Norway, Sweden, Finland and Russia. It rarely arrives in Britain before mid-November.

Index

(The numerals in italic type refer to the *figure numbers* of illustrations)